Introduction to innovation

Volume 2

Entrepreneurship and innovation

Jon-Arild Johannessen (Ed.)

Copyright © 2016 Author Name

All rights reserved.

ISBN-13:
978-1536998719

ISBN-10:
1536998710

FOREWORD

Chapter 1 and 2 are written by Stokvik, H., Adriaenssen, D. & Johannessen, J-A.

Chapter 3 is written by by Stokvik, H., Adriaenssen, D.; Johannessen, J-A. & Sætesdal, H.

Chapter 4 is written by Stokvik, H., Adriaenssen, D.; Johannessen, J-A. & Skålsvik, H.

Chapter 5 is written by Stokvik, H., Adriaenssen, D. & Johannessen, J-A.

CONTENTS

Chapter 1 Strategic entrepreneurship 6

Chapter 2 Managing knowledge resources 48

Chapter 3 Knowledge management and innovation 92

Chapter 4 Innovation and entrepreneurial policy 128

Chapter 5 New venture creation 162

ABOUT THE AUTHORS 198

Chapter 1 Strategic entrepreneurship

Introduction

The importance of entrepreneurship in established organizations has grown significantly in the last decades (Høglund, 2015), and is highlighted in the special issue of Strategic Entrepreneurship Journal (Demil, et.al., 2015:1-11) . Strategic entrepreneurship is distinct from small business management (Wickham, 2006). It is a new concept, which fuses the concept of entrepreneurship and strategic management (Hitt, et.al., 2002). The new concept may be though of as a new way of thinking about entrepreneurship in established organizations (Hitt, Camp & Ireland, 2002), for instance like a knowledge spillover theory. In the knowledge spillover theory one may think of organizations as a system of different types of knowledge (Ferreira et al, 2016). Thus the question arises as to what constitutes strategic entrepreneurship (Luke, 2008).

We will in this chapter use aspects of -risk, value-creation and knowledge processes to show aspects of strategic entrepreneurship. We will also show the distinction between strategic management and strategic entrepreneurship. Our investigation will focus how strategic entrepreneurship can increase intrapreneurial intensity. It is not the case that an organization is either intrapreneurial or not, but rather that there is a degree of intrapreneurial intensity in any organization (Luke, 2008). Even in the most bureaucratic and conservative organizations, there will always be a certain level of intrapreneurial intensity, although it may be difficult for an outsider to see the visible results of these activities and processes (Ferreira, et. Al., 2016).

First we introduce the knowledge foundation of the chapter.

Knowledge foundation

Schumpeter's entrepreneur can operate inside an enterprise or independently (Andersen, 2009; 2011). He writes, "The carrying out of new combinations, the individuals whose function is to carry them out we call entrepreneurs" (1934: 74-75), and they are: "all who actually fulfil the function by which we define the concept, even if they are, as is becoming the rule, dependent employees of a company" (op. cit.).

The early Schumpeter (1934) was concerned with independent entrepreneurs, i.e. entrepreneurs who establish an enterprise outside established organizations, referred to as "Schumpeter Mark I". The later Schumpeter (1942) was more concerned with organizational entrepreneurship and the innovative entrepreneur, also known as "Schumpeter Mark II" (see Utterback, 1994:193).

Consequently, in this context, it appears that the link between innovation and entrepreneurship has an early theoretical foundation.

In practice, both innovation and entrepreneurship are related to creative processes and value creation. Independent entrepreneurs may work in teams; they may be novices or people with a lot of experience; and they may start up a business without having any connection to an existing business (see Sharma & Chrisma, 1999: 17; Westhead, et al., 2003). While these innovative entrepreneurs drive the market out of equilibrium, (Schumpeter, 1934), "classical" entrepreneurs restore the market back to equilibrium (see Kirzner, 1973).

There are two main branches of research on entrepreneurship; the first examines the individual entrepreneur who independently starts a business. This area of research has its historical roots in the early Schumpeter (Andersen, 2011). The second area of research is concerned with how entrepreneurship is fostered in established organizations (Andersen, 2009); this is often described as intrapreneurship, and, amongst others, finds its theoretical foundation in Burgelman (1983a, 1983b). Intrapreneurship and strategic entrepreneurship are closely related but distinct concepts. Strategic entrepreneurship may be considered as a process of influence, where the purpose is to reveal, discover or create opportunities, and then evaluate and exploit them (see Finkelstein & Hambrick, 1996; Shane & Venkataraman, 2000).

Value creation in this context is closely related to Schumpeter's concept of creative destruction, because even if something is destroyed in the innovation process, value is created in other places, i.e. where something new and creative is flourishing. "Value" refers to the system of the activities and processes that meet human needs. The concept of strategic entrepreneurship relates to entrepreneurship's strategic position. Strategic entrepreneurship is concerned with discovering and exploiting opportunities within and beyond an organization, in order to promote value creation (Venkataraman & Sarasvathy, 2001, Ireland et al., 2003). Strategic entrepreneurship may be understood as the link between entrepreneurship and strategic thinking (Hitt et al., 2001).

The chapter asks the following question: How can the various aspects of strategic entrepreneurship provide us with more insight into intrapreneurial intensity?

There are three aspects of the research question we will investigate further:

1. How is risk related to strategic entrepreneurship and intrapreneurial intensity?
2. How is knowledge processes related to strategic entrepreneurship and intrapreneurial intensity?
3. How is value creation related to strategic entrepreneurship and intrapreneurial intensity

Figures 1 shows a conceptual model that illustrates aspects of strategic entrepreneurship.

Figure 1: Aspects of strategic entrepreneurship

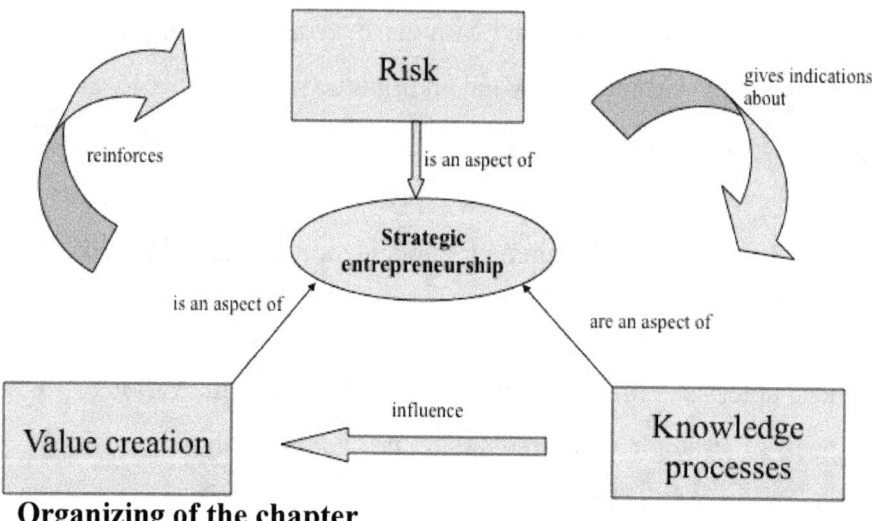

Organizing of the chapter

The chapter is structured in relation to Figure 1. First, strategic entrepreneurship is discussed. Secondly, strategic entrepreneurship is discussed from a risk perspective. Third, knowledge processes are discussed in relation to strategic entrepreneurship. Finally, strategic entrepreneurship is discussed from a value creation perspective. In the onclusion: Policy implications for strategic entrepreneurship is examined on the basis of the concept intrapreneurial intensity.

Strategic entrepreneurship and intrapreneurial intensity

Entrepreneurship may be understood as the processes in which "opportunities to create future goods and services are discovered, evaluated and exploited" (Shane & Venkaturaman, 2000: 218). Some of the enterprises the entrepreneur engages in are innovative, while others are not. Some enterprises are started up independently of other organizations, while others occur within established organizations. While established organizations may be adept at creating competitive advantages, they are less skilled at developing new opportunities, say Ireland, et al. (2003). However, it is the development of new opportunities that is crucial to the idea of strategic entrepreneurship.

Strategic entrepreneurship concerns discovering and exploiting opportunities, while strategic management is related to creating sustainable competitive advantages (see Venkataraman & Sarasvathy, 2001, Hitt, et al., 2005). Strategic entrepreneurship is important for both entrepreneurs and intrapreneurs.
Entrepreneurship is divided here into classic entrepreneurship and innovative entrepreneurship. Intrapreneurship is divided into "corporate" entrepreneurship and "corporate venturing".
"Corporate" entrepreneurship may be understood as the system of a company's innovative processes, its willingness to take risks, as

well as its proactive behaviour (Miller, 1983). We see a clear connection between "corporate" entrepreneurship and Gratton's term (2007) of "hot spot[s]" in companies. "Corporate" entrepreneurship has proven to be very important for both financial and non-financial performance (Zahra, et al., 1999). "Corporate venturing" concerns the process by which a company enters new markets (Venkataraman, et al., 1992). This process may be internal or external. External processes here are related to alliances and acquisitions. Internal "corporate venturing" is synonymous here with "corporate" entrepreneurship (intrapreneurship) (Scholthammer, 1982).

Pinchot (1985) coined the phrase intrapreneur in order to focus on internal entrepreneurship in organizations. However, we also make the distinction here between innovative intrapreneurship and classical intrapreneurship. This classification is consistent with Zahra (1995) who uses the term incubation activities, where we use the term innovative intrapreneurship (for pedagogical reasons).

Entrepreneurs and intrapreneurs transform knowledge into new opportunities. Recent research shows that it is the human resources that the entrepreneur and intrapreneur possess which are essential for success, rather than their financial resources, although the latter are obviously important (see Heneman, et al., 2000; Brush, et al., 2001). Their human resources are linked to knowledge processes and leadership.

Entrepreneurial leadership, or what we term here strategic entrepreneurship, is described by McGrath & MacMillan (2000) as the main resource in an organization. This type of leadership has no official function in an organizational hierarchy. Entrepreneurial leadership may be practiced by many people in an organization, and consists of persons who alone, or together with others, create the "hot spots" in organizations (Gratton, 2007) referred to above. A "hot spot" may briefly be described as the centre of the creative energy fields in an organization, where new ideas are developed and put into practice in order to promote economic growth. The result of these creative energy fields is a high degree of intrapreneurial activity (Morris, 1998), which may be used to measure the extent of strategic entrepreneurship. The level of intrapreneurial intensity may be understood in relation to the number of "hot spots" in an organization.

The management of creative fields may be considered as the dominant logic that must exist in an organization if it is to promote intrapreneurial intensity. The dominant logic is the system of prevailing mental models or maps, which guide the way of thinking in an organization (see Prahalad & Bettis, 1986: 485). Without this dominant logic in an organization, there will be a movement towards bureaucratization and rigidity, which may result in the organization's becoming prey to the destructive element of Schumpeter's "creative destruction".

Assumption 1: If organizations aim to promote strategic

entrepreneurship and intrapreneurial intensity, they must develop "hot spots".

Consequence: Organizations that intend to develop strategic entrepreneurship must be based on the development and distribution of highly creative teams.

Strategic entrepreneurship and strategic management are related but distinct concepts; they are related in the sense that top management must retain control. However, they are distinct in their outcomes. Strategic management focuses largely on long-term competitive advantages (Hitt, et al., 2002; 2005). Strategic entrepreneurship focuses on organizational entrepreneurship and intrapreneurial intensity (Ireland, et al., 2003; Gratton, 2007; Morris, 1998). The main focus of strategic entrepreneurship is to identify and exploit new opportunities for value creation (Venkataraman & Sarasvathy, 2001). Strategic management and strategic entrepreneurship differ in focus, and partly in relation to results. For instance, it is not a condition of strategic management that it must develop an entrepreneurship culture in an organization. However, it is an absolute condition of strategic entrepreneurship that management encourages and participates in driving forward an entrepreneurial culture in the organization (Alvanez & Barney, 2002). An entrepreneurial culture is: "one in which new ideas and creativity are expected, risk taking is encouraged, failure is tolerated, learning is promoted, product, process and administrative innovativeness are championed, and continuous change is viewed as a conveyor of opportunities" (Ireland, et al., 2003: 975). To develop this kind of entrepreneurial culture is not a necessary condition for strategic management; a situation may occur in strategic management where entrepreneurship and innovation must be limited; this will never occur in entrepreneurship-related development. In other words, strategic management and strategic entrepreneurship represent two different ways of thinking.

Although there is no great similarity between the two ways of thinking, Venkataraman & Sarasvathy (2001) attempt to integrate them by using an analogy to Shakespeare's *Romeo and Juliet*. Strategic entrepreneurship, they say, is like Romeo without a Juliet on the balcony; and strategic management is like Juliet on the balcony without a Romeo. Although the comparison is interesting, it lacks a significant element, namely, an analogy to the final scene of the play. They argue that the integration of strategic management and strategic entrepreneurship is analogous to Romeo meeting Juliet in the sense that "love" will flower. However, if we follow the analogy to the final scene then the meeting (or integration) will end in the death of both. It seems that Venkataraman & Sarasvathy (2001) have chosen to ignore the final scene in order to fit the analogy to their way of thinking. However, if we follow Shakespeare's text more faithfully, the result of the meeting of the two will result in the worst situation imaginable. In other words, we believe that strategic entrepreneurship and strategic entrepreneurship should be allowed to exist independently of each other in an organization, and not be integrated.

Assumption 2: If an organization aims to develop strategic entrepreneurship and increase intrapreneurial intensity, it should develop an intrapreneurial culture.

Consequence 1: Organizations need to distinguish between strategic management and strategic entrepreneurship.

Consequence 2: Organizations need to scale up strategic entrepreneurship so that it is on the same functional level as strategic management.

How is risk related to strategic entrepreneurship and intrapreneurial intensity?

Opportunities create both uncertainty and risk. Uncertainty can to a certain extent be clarified by obtaining additional information. Risk presupposes knowledge. This distinction between risk and uncertainty related to entrepreneurship activities was first highlighted by Knight in 1921[1].

Risk is the trigger effect that encourages the entrepreneur to act. Where others retreat, the entrepreneur goes forth and puts all his/her heart into it, because he/she is challenged by taking risks and the potential rewards that lie at the end of the road.

Entrepreneurs and intrapreneurs are experts in dealing with risks and interpreting risk maps, which describe the uncertainty that exists in the external world (Foester, 1986). Skilled entrepreneurs and intrapreneurs are able to discern patterns in uncertainty and place themselves where the potential reward is greatest. It is reasonable to assume that it is not chance or luck that causes one person to succeed where many others fail. In other words, those who succeed are able to see patterns others are unable to see. A pattern in this context is always something that is not visible on the surface, but rather something "beneath the surface", which skilled entrepreneurs and intrapreneurs are able to interpret. They are able to see opportunities where others see only hindrances. This is where strategic entrepreneurship is important – employing pattern recognition and mental risk maps.

---

[1] Risk is an epistemological construct, while uncertainty is an ontological construct. One obtains information about uncertainty from the external world.

The inexperienced entrepreneur and intrapreneur are unable to discern these patterns. They develop business plans, create strategies and take the necessary time to apply for funding through public and other channels (funding agencies require the submission of such plans). Time passes, of course, and the scope of opportunities may change in the meantime. Although the business plans and strategies may be well drafted, they are less applicable once the scope of opportunities has changed or disappeared. In other words, when the rate of change is great business plans and strategies rarely coincide with emerging opportunities. Thus, when the plans and strategies are finally implemented, the scope of opportunities has often changed: the plans and strategies thus become historical documents of only peripheral interest.

Entrepreneurial activities involve the use of mental maps of risk and insight into patterns to varying degrees. The approaches chosen will also differentiate the accomplished entrepreneur and intrapreneur from those less skilled and experienced. The use of mental risk maps and skills in pattern recognition are closely related to strategic entrepreneurship.

Mental risk maps and pattern recognition are essential at a time when the rate of change and turbulence is great; when this is not the case, it may be appropriate to apply business plans and strategies to a greater extent.

When the rate of change and turbulence is great, and there is consequently considerable uncertainty, accumulated experience will become less useful when adapting to a new and unknown situation. However, it may be possible to "create" one's own future and that of others by acting on the basis of ideas and perceptions (but not accumulated experience).

When acting on the basis of ideas and perceptions, reality will be "constructed", because the entrepreneur and intrapreneur have chosen to select some elements while discarding others. Therefore, the mental risk map that is developed will be simultaneously both dynamic and flexible; dynamic in relation to one's adapting to what has been selected, and flexible in that certain aspects of the ideas and perceptions have been discarded.

This dynamic flexibility involves shutting out parts of the scope of opportunities, thus establishing a "studio" in which the entrepreneur and intrapreneur are able to develop their ideas in the limited scope of opportunities they have created by selecting some elements from the external world, while discarding others. It is in this limited scope of opportunities that strategic entrepreneurship emerges, which to some extent is influenced by Schoemaker (2002), Courtney (2001) and DeMeyer, et al., (2002).

When mental risk maps are developed it is important to be aware that we tend to underestimate risk, although we may be aware of it (Kahneman & Lovallo, 1993). Scenario thinking, training and planning may be one way to deal with risk, by taking into account the possible underestimation of risk (Van der Heijde, 1996; Sterman, 2000).

A simplification of Knight's (1921) understanding of risk may be described as a function of three dimensions: exposure, rewards and time. If we take into consideration Kahneman & Lovallo's (1993) insights concerning the underestimation of risk, together with Knight's concept of risk, and relate this to the entrepreneur as a constant factor regarding the search for new opportunities, then risk may be theoretically understood as a potential downside and corresponding lack of upside in relation to rewards and time. The point here is that we tend to overestimate the upsides and underestimate the downsides of risk in relation to entrepreneurial activities (Kahneman & Lovallo, 1993). When this happens, the scope of opportunities will be greater than it ought to be from the perspective of risk assessment. In practice this means that our mental risk maps have a tendency to amplify risk simply due to the way they are constituted, which may be understood when we consider Kahneman & Lovallo's (1993) insights.

Exposure can be reduced by making adjustments to risk models when the rate of change increases. This involves a procedure whereby one first tests the model, then operates the model in practice, and then re-tests the model again before implementing the project. This may be understood as the scientific model TOTE (test, operate, test, execute). This model may be used by the entrepreneur and intrapreneur to reduce risk when the rate of change is great, thus minimizing the tendency to overestimate the upside and underestimate the downside. In this way, strategic entrepreneurship is related to the scientific TOTE model.

In Figure 2 we have constructed what we choose to term risk maps.

Fig. 2 Risk maps

	Small	Large
Strategic	Business strategies	Insight into patterns
Operative	Business plans	Mental risk maps

Level — Rate of change

Proposition 1: If the rate of change in the external world is great, then risks are high, and business plans and business strategies will be counterproductive.

Consequence: If the rate of change is great, the entrepreneur and intrapreneur ought to be evaluated on the basis of their fundamental ideas, and their personal qualities, i.e. their mental risk maps and their insight into patterns. If this happens, then intrapreneurial intensity will emerge.

No matter how we view strategic entrepreneurship, it is generally agreed that risks are taken in order to gain advantages. This is an extension of North's action theory (1968, 1981, 1990; 1993; 1994; 1996; 1997) and Asplund's (2010) motivation theory. North's action theory is, in short, that one acts on the basis of the system of rewards in the institutional framework which one is a part of. Asplund's motivation theory is, in short, that one is motivated by social responses.

Proposition 2: If an organization aims to foster strategic entrepreneurship and increase intrapreneurial intensity, the system of rewards in the organization's culture must reflect this.

Consequence: People are motivated by the relationship between social responses and reward systems, which in turn relates to the norms and values of a culture.

How is knowledge processes related to strategic entrepreneurship and intrapreneurial intensity?

Schumpeter's entrepreneurs are not the ones that create new inventions; these people he calls "inventors". Schumpeter's entrepreneur is an innovator in the sense that he/she "is carrying out --- new combinations" (1934: 75). The creative knowledge process that leads to an invention belongs to the domain of innovation, while the creative process of knowledge as "carrying out new combinations" belongs to the entrepreneurial domain. Both knowledge processes are integrated, however, in the value creation process.

Schumpeter (1934: 88-89) says of the entrepreneur: "Although entrepreneurs may be inventors…they are inventors not by nature of their function…" The entrepreneur is more like an "implementer" who seizes an opportunity, combining and utilising various areas of knowledge in order to create value. The entrepreneur is always looking for new opportunities to create value; he/she "carries out new combinations" (Schumpeter, 1934: 78). The result of the entrepreneur's activities and processes is creative destruction: "This process of creative destructions is the essential fact about capitalism", Schumpeter argues (1942: 83).

Innovation and entrepreneurship are integrated through value creation. The creative process is the basis of both entrepreneurship and innovation, and value creation is the end result for both of these processes.

In the same way that Schumpeter says (1942: 133), that innovation can easily be reduced to a routine, and thereby inhibit creative processes, entrepreneurship may be reduced to "bureaucracy", and reduce creative processes as well. Routinization and bureaucratization are the innovative and entrepreneurial paradox. It is an offspring of the philosopher Zapfe's paradox that seems to occur: in other words, that which one is good at, becomes one's downfall. This entrepreneurial assassination has in recent times been described by Chandler (1962: 12) and Greiner (1972) amongst others, in addition to Schumpeter (1942).

Innovation and entrepreneurship become integrated through the creative process. This process may easily be dampened and disrupted through routines, procedures, bureaucracy, rigid structures and predictable processes. The reason is that the creative process always operates along the boundaries of established knowledge (see Kanter, 1985: 138; Kanter, 2006); this knowledge is here called hidden knowledge. This is an area where "you do not know what you do not know". Kirzner expresses this as: "Entrepreneurial profit opportunities exist where people do not know what they do not know, and do not know that they do not know it" (Kirzner, 1982: 273). Hidden knowledge may be understood as the theoretical knowledge foundation for creativity, entrepreneurship and innovation.

That which one does not know what one knows is related to tacit knowledge (Polanyi, 2009). That which one knows is often referred to as explicit knowledge (Collins, 2010). That which one knows what one does not know is defined as the domain of research (Collins & Evans, 2009).

In Figure 3 we have constructed what we choose to term the knowledge window.

Figure 3: The knowledge window

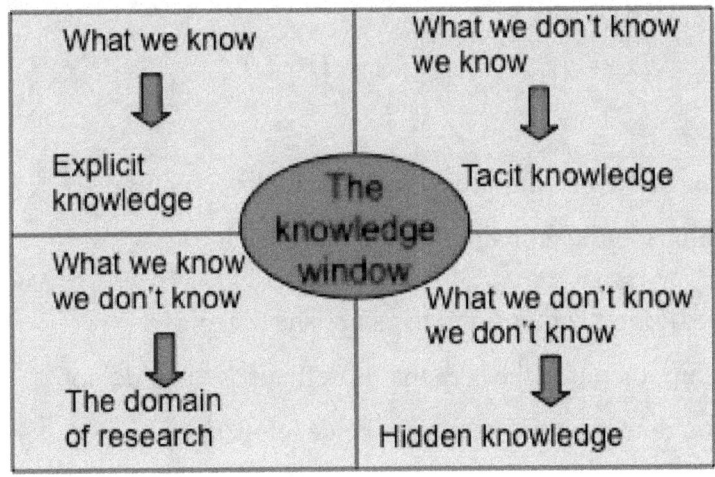

It is in this knowledge window that strategic entrepreneurship takes place. In all four domains of knowledge there are opportunities which strategic entrepreneurship is able to use. However, it is mainly in the domain of hidden knowledge that entrepreneurial opportunities occur; this is where strategic entrepreneurship should concentrate its focus.

There are many indications that the development of simple risk maps based on risk strategies has positive consequences for the entrepreneur. Increased revenues that exceed expectations by 35-45% and reduced costs of 15-45% have been reported (see Carter, et al., 1996). One of the explanations may be that the entrepreneurs' mental risk maps are harmonised with the uncertainty of the external world, and the tendency to underestimate risks documented by Kahneman & Lovallo (1993) is clarified to a greater extent.

Proposition 3: Strategic entrepreneurship and intrapreneurial intensity develops in the domain of hidden knowledge.

Consequence: If organizations aim to establish strategic entrepreneurship, then it is the area that is defined as "you do not know what you do not know" that must be developed.

How is value creation related to strategic entrepreneurship and intrapreneurial intensity?

Entrepreneurship and innovation create two separate processes in the economy. Entrepreneurship fills gaps in the market and pushes the economy towards equilibrium. Innovation often results in creative destruction that leads to disequilibrium. Both processes, however, foster value creation (see Bruyat & Julien, 2000). Value creation, though, leads to value destruction for some, through the destructive processes which are a practical consequence of Schumpeter's creative destruction.

Value creation is central to the understanding of both entrepreneurship and innovation, because it is the goal of both processes. But what is meant exactly by the term value creation?

One meaning of value creation may be understood from different perspectives. On the most general level, one may consider it to be the value of all the activities and processes that meet human needs. At the system level, one may consider value creation as those results that benefit, financially and non-financially, the members of the system in question and the environment (see Habbershon, et al., 2003). At the individual level, one can say that value creation is any outcome that increases an individual's well being.

The activities and processes that are the prerequisites for economic growth are referred to by Porter (1980, 1985) as the value chain. Stabell & Fjellstad (1998) term the processes value network and value shop. Johannessen et.al., (1997;1999) term the processes value community and value dialogue. All these five types of processes – value- chain, value-network, value-shop, the value-community and the value-dialogue, are all assumed to be important for understanding value creation in the global knowledge economy.

Within the academic literature on strategy in the 1980s and to some extent the 1990s there is a strong focus on the value chain. In particular, this was reflected in Michael Porter's books (1980;1985; 1990; 1996; 2004). Value chain thinking has focused on a linear and sequential understanding of value creation. This school of thought defines value creation as consisting of inbound logistics, operations, outbound logistics, marketing/sales and service. At the business level, value chain thinking has been linked to a linear understanding related to supplier - customer activities. From this perspective, value chain thinking is closely related to strategic management.

Value chain thinking has been increasingly criticized in recent years (e.g. Stabell & Fjellstad, 1998). The first wave of criticism argued that value chain thinking was only suitable for describing and understanding traditional manufacturing companies, and could not be applied to the same extent when examining knowledge production. Further criticism pointed out that a linear understanding, for instance at the level of a business, is rarely valid. We therefore now see a stronger emphasis on "prosumer systems" (Toffler 1980), where suppliers, businesses and customers are seen as a holistic system, continually interacting. Various types of companies will, however, have a different emphasis on the different types of value creation processes, as well as all the processes which are to be found (or should be found) in most businesses. This means that the value chain is still relevant;

however, one must also simultaneously focus on other value creation processes.

Within traditional manufacturing companies the value chain has focused on the transformation of materials into some product, whereas the focus for most businesses in the knowledge economy is related to the transformation of information into knowledge. In other words, the transformation of materials is not the central focus in the knowledge economy, although it is often systemically linked to knowledge processes.

In a world that increasingly emphasizes the flexibility of a modular logic (Garud, et.al., 2002) information, knowledge and communication are key elements in relation to the value chain (Brynjolfsson & McAfee, 2014). The value chain transforms raw-materials, data, information and knowledge, amongst other things, into output consisting of components that can be assembled into solutions to satisfy customer demands. This type of economy can be compared to one composed of Lego parts; these Lego parts are assembled in relation to a cost, quality, skills and innovation logic in the global knowledge economy (Baird & Henderson, 2001; Brynjolfsson & McAfee, 2014; Haag, et.al., 2012)

Within the value network the focus is on communication and external relations (Stabell & Fjellstad, 1998). Primarily, this communication is targeted at customers, but it is also aimed at suppliers, competitors, etc. While the value chain focuses on information, the value network focuses on communication. But, both value creation processes – the value chain and the value network – operate mainly in relation to an industrial logic (Porter, 1980;1985;1990; 1996; Stabell & Fjellstad, 1998). One can say that while value chain thinking is closely related to strategic management, the value network is more closely related to strategic logistics (Dittman, 2012). In order to create value for customers through communication, an important feature of the value network is the coordination and integration of information. Roughly speaking, one can say that the value network receives information about the solution elements from the value chain. This information is coordinated and integrated by the value network to provide value to customers through customer solutions.

The value shop operates within a knowledge-logic, and is committed to facilitating efficient performance at the operational level. This means first and foremost ensuring that the operational level has access to resources, and an organization of operations that contributes to an efficient utilization of these resources. The value shop is closely related to strategic competence development (Tidd, 2012). This means skills related to both material and immaterial resources, but with a strong emphasis on immaterial resources. Immaterial resources are primarily related to the knowledge, skills and attitudes required for efficient operation. Somewhat simplified, one can argue that the value shop receives information from the operational level, value chain and value network, and ensures that they have access to the necessary expertise resources for efficient operation. Operational efficiency is understood here as a focus on productivity.

The value community is based on the organization's needs regarding communication with the external world and the organization's external legitimacy and reputation. This implies an emphasis on value creation processes related to the values, norms and attitudes which are communicated externally; these may include social responsibility, the third bottom line, ethics, etc. Reputation and reputation management are critical processes in the value community. The value community may be understood as strategic corporate social responsibility (Werther & Chandler, 2010).

The value dialogue focuses primarily on creativity, innovation, new ideas, etc; success in this instance requires a focus on both information and communication. The value dialogue is the area of business where the scope of opportunity unfolds. It is also here that mental risk maps are developed and transformed into value for an organization, i.e. strategic entrepreneurship is linked to the value dialogue.

The implications for strategic entrepreneurship of the five value creation processes are to be found in any organization in the knowledge economy. Some organizations, however, will have a greater emphasis on one or several of the five value creation processes. However, it is our view that all five value creation processes must be fostered, if an organization is to be viable in the global knowledge economy. The course of action that forms the basis of this analysis is that organizations in the knowledge economy must have a greater degree of variation internally than externally, which is a simplified rewriting of "the law of requisite variety" (Ashby, 1956). Consequently it is reasonable to assume that the five value creation processes must exist in every organization in the global knowledge economy, if the organization is to be a viable one. We have illustrated the five value creation processes and their focus on strategy in Figure 4.

Figure 4: The five value creation processes

Proposition 4: It is primarily within the value dialogue that strategic entrepreneurship unfolds.

Consequence 1: It is within the value dialogue that the scope of opportunities for the creative and new emerges, and it is here the potensial for intrapreneurial intensity is to be found.

Proposition 5: If an organization finds a balance between the five value creation processes, it will develop strategic entrepreneurship within the organization and increase intrapreneurial intensity.

Consequence: In the knowledge economy the focus should be on promoting the productivity of knowledge workers, because they will develop strategic entrepreneurship and increase intrapreneurial intensity.

Conclusion

The research question was: How can the various aspects of strategic entrepreneurship provide us with more insight into intrapreneurial intensity?

The answer is linked to the assumptions and propositions developed in the chapter. The theory that emerges through the system of propositions set out in this chapter is the outline of a theory for the development of strategic entrepreneurship and intrapreneurial intensity in organizations.

Policy implications for strategic entrepreneurship and intrapreneurial intensity.

As mentioned above, Gratton (2007) has shown that it is possible to identify zones of creative energy fields (hot spots) in all types of organizations.

We call the degree of intrapreneurship here "intrapreneurial intensity". We have constructed intrapreneurial intensity on the basis of two main dimensions. One is connected to the frequency of creative energy fields (hot spots) in an organization. The second is the degree of innovation in relation to products, services and processes. The idea of using the degree of innovation to establish the type of intrapreneurship in an organization may also be found in Krieser et al. (2002). Others have used both risk and productivity to evaluate the degree of intrapreneurship (Covin & Slevin, 1989). We incorporate risk and productivity in the concept of 'degree of innovation', because a higher degree of innovation will mean that an organization takes greater risks. Similarly, a low level of innovation involves a low degree of risk.

Intrapreneurial intensity in an organization may be described as a function of creative energy fields and the degree of innovation. Both of these dimensions (constructs) can be operationalized. We describe four types of intrapreneurial intensity, as illustrated in Figure 5. Intrapreneurial intensity indicates the level of activity in the value dialogue and the level of strategic entrepreneurship within an organization.

Figure 5: strategic entrepreneurship and intrapreneurial intensity

	Small	Large
Many creative energy fields ("hot spots") in an organization	Dynamic intrapreneurship	Revolutionary intrapreneurship
Few	Sporadic intrapreneurship	Radical intrapreneurship

Degree of intrapreneurship

Organizations with a flatter structure have a greater degree of intrapreneurial intensity than those with a bureaucratic and hierarchical structure (Zahra & Covin, 1995). Organizations that balance individual and team performances will also have a larger degree of intrapreneurial intensity (Morris, et al., 1994). Research also supports the idea that a certain degree of flexible resources promotes intrapreneurial intensity (Morris & Jones, 1993). It is also suggested by Miles (2005: 93) that when the organizational assessment emphasizes innovation and risk, intrapreneurial intensity increases. We also know that when job descriptions are relatively broad, this may also promote intrapreneurial intensity (Miles, 2005). A good deal of research supports the hypothesis that the stronger the degree of market orientation an organization has, the greater the intrapreneurial intensity (see Miles & Arnold, 1991).

An obvious question in this discussion is: Do organizations with greater intrapreneurial intensity perform better than organizations with lower levels of intrapreneurial intensity? Morris, who has done a great deal of research in this area, says: "The answer is an unequivocal yes" (Morris & Kuratko, 2002: 53). However, further research is required to examine empirically the propositions that are presented here .

References

Alvarez, S.A. & Barney, J.B. (2002). "Resource-based theory and the entrepreneurial firm", in Hitt, M.A., Ireland, R.D.; Camp, S.M. & Sexton, D.L. (Ed.). Strategic Entrepreneurship: Creating a New Mindset, Blackwell, Oxford, pp. 89-105.

Andersen, E. (2009). Schumpeter's Evolutionary Economics: A

Theoretical, Historical and Statistical Analysis of the Engine of Capitalism, Anthem Press, London.

Andersen, E.S (2011). Joseph A. Schumpeter: A Theory of Social and Economic Evolution (Great Thinkers in Economics), Palgrave, London.

Ashby, W. R. (1956). An Introduction to Cybernetics, Chapman, London.

Asplund, J. (2010). Det sociala livets elementära former, Korpen, Stockholm.

Baird, L. & Henderson, J.C. (2001). The Knowledge Engine, Berrett-Koehler, San Francisco.

Baumeister, R.F. (2012). Willpower, Allen Lane, London.

Brush, C.G.; Greene, P.G. & Hart, M.M. (2001). "From initial idea to unique advantage: The entrepreneurial challenge of constructing a resource base", Academy of Management Executive, 15, 1: 64-80.

Bruyat, C. & Julien, P.A. (2000). "Defining the field of research in entrepreneurship", Journal of Business Venturing, 16: 165-180.

Brynjolfsson, E. & McAfee, A. (2014). The Second Machine Age, W.W. Noron, New York.

Bunge, M. (1977). Treatise on basic philosophy. Vol. 3. Ontology I: The furniture of the world. Dordrecht, Holland: D. Reidel.

Bunge, M. **(1985).** Philosophy of Science and Technology, Part I, Reidel, Dordrecht.

Bunge, M. **(1998).** Philosophy of science: From problem to theory, Volume one, Transaction Publishers, New Jersey.

Burgelman, R.A. **(1983a).** "A process model of internal corporate venturing in the divesified major firm", Administrative Science Quarterly, 28, 2: 223-244.

Burgelman, R.A. **(1983b).** "Corporate entrepreneurship and strategic management: Insights from a process study", Management Science, 29: 1349-1364.

Burt, R.S. **(1992).** Structural holes: The Social Structure of Complexity, Harvard University Press, Boston, MA.

Carter, J.; VanDijk, M. & Gibson, K. **(1996).** "Capital investment: How not to build the Titanic", McKinsey Quarterly, 4: 147-159.

Chandler, A.D. **(1962).** Strategy and Structure, MIT Press, cambridge, MA.

Collins, H. **(2010).** Tacit and Explicit knowledge, University of Chicago Press, Chicago.

Collins, H. & Evans, R. **(2009).** Rethinking Expertise, University of Chicago Press, Chicago.

Cooper, A.; Dunkelberg, W.C.; Woo, C.Y. & Dennis, W.

(1990). "New business in America: The firms and their owners", NFIB Foundation, Washington, DC.

Courtney, H. (2001). 20/20 Forsight, Harvard Business School Press, Boston, MA.

Covin, J.G. & Slevin, D.P. (1989). "Strategic management of small firms in hostile behaviour", Entrepreneurship: Theory and Practice, 16: 7-25.

DeMeyer, A.; Loch, C.H. & Pich, M.T. (2002). "Managing project uncertainty: From variations to chaos", Sloan management Review, 43, 2: 60-67.

Demil, B.; lecocq, X.; Ricart, J.E. & Zott, C. (2015). Introduction to the SEJ special issue on business models: Business models within the domain of strategic entrepreneurship, 9, 1:1-11.

Dittman, J.P. (2012). Supply Chain Transformation: Building and Executing an Integrated Supply Chain Strategy, McGraw-Hill, New York.

Drucker, P.F. (1999). "Knowledge worker productivity: The biggest challenge", California Management Review, 41, 2: 79-94.

Drucker, P.F. (1999a). Management Challenges for the 21st Century, Harper, New York.

Fereira, J.J.; Dana, L. & Ratten, V. (2016). Knowledge spillover based strategic entrepreneurship, Routledge, London.

Finkelstein, S. & Hambrick, D. (1996). Strategic leadership: Top Excecutives and their Effects on Organizations, West, St. Paul, M.N.

Foester, R. (1986). Innovation: The Attackers Advantage, Summit Books, New York.

Garud, R.; Kumaraswamy, A. &,Langlois, R. (2002). Managing in the Modular Age: New Perspectives on Architectures, Networks and Organizations, Wiley-Blackwell, New York.

Gratton, L. (2007). Hot Spots, Prentice Hall, New York.

Greiner, L.E. (1972). Evolution and Revolution as Organizations grow, Harvard Business Review, 50: 37-46.

Haag, S.; Cummings, M.; McCubbrey, D.; Pinsonneault, A.; Donovan, R. (2012). Management Information Systems for the Information Age, McGraw Hill, Ryerson.

Habbershon, T.; Williams, M. & MacMillan, I. (2003). "A unified systems perspective of family, firm performance", Journal of Business Venturing, 18, 4: 451-465.

Heneman, R.L.; Tansky, J.W. & Camp, S.M. (2000). "Human resource practices in small and medium size enterprises: Unaswered questions and future research perspectives", Entrepreneurship, Theory and Practice, 25, 1: 1-16.

Herbst, R.F. & Link, A.N. (1988). The Entrepreneur, Praeger, New York.

Hitt, M.A.; Ireland, R.D.; Camp, S.M. & Sexton, D.L. (2001). "Strategic entrepreneurship: Entrepreneurial strategies for wealth creation", Strategic Management Journal, 22: 479-491.

Hitt, M.A.; Camp, S.M. & Ireland, R.D.; (2002). Strategic entrepreneurship: Creating a new mindset, John Wiley & Sons, New York

Hitt, M.A.; Ireland, R.D.; Camp, S.M. & Sexton, D.L. (2002). "Strategic entrepreneurship: Integrating entrepreneurial and strategic management", in Hitt, M.A.; Ireland, R.D.; Camp, S.M. & Sexton, D.L. (Ed.). Strategic Entrepreneurship, Creating a New Mindset, Blackwell, Oxford.

Hitt, M.A.; Ireland, R.D. & Hoskisson, R.E. (2005). "Strategic management: Competitiveness and globalization", South Western Publishing, Cincinnati, OH.

Høglund, L. (2015). Strategic entrepreneurship, Studentlitteratur, AB., Stockholm.

Ireland, R.D.; Hitt, M.A.; Simon, D.G. (2003). "A model of strategic entrepreneurship: The construct and its dimensions", Journal of Management, xx:963-989.

Johannessen, J-A.; Olsen, B. & Olaisen, J. (1997). Organizing for innovation, Long Range Planning, 30, 1:96-109.

Johannessen, J-A.; Olaisen, J. & Olsen, B. (1999). Managing and organizing innovation in the knowledge economy, European Journal of Innovation Management, Vol. 2 Iss: 3, pp.116 – 12.

Kahneman, D. & Lovallo, D. (1993). "Timid choices and bold forecasts: A cognitive perspective on risktaking", Management Science, 39,1: 17-31.

Kanter, R.M. (1985). The Change Masters, Routledge, London.

Kanter, R. M. (2006). "From cells to communities: Deconstructing the organization, in Gallos, J.V. (Ed.). Organization Development, Jossey Bass, San Francisco, pp. 858-888.

Kirzner, I.M. (1973). Competitive Entrepreneurship, University of Chicago Press, Chicago.

Kirzner, S. (1982). "The theory of entrepreneurship in economic growth", in Kent, C.A.; Sexton, D.L. & Vesper, K.H. (Ed.). Encyclopedia of Entrepreneurship, Prentice Hall, Englewood Cliffs, NJ.

Knight, F.H. (1921). Risk, Uncertainty and Profit, University of Chicago Press, Chicago.

Krieser, P.M.; Marino, L.D. & Weaver, K.M. (2002). "Assessing the psychometric properties of the entrepreneurial orientation scale", Entrepreneurship: Theory and Practice, 26, 4:

71-94.

Luke, B. (2008). Uncovering strategic entrepreneurship: An examination of theory and practice, VDM Verlag Dr. Müller, London/Berlin.

McGrath, R. & MacMillan, I. (2000). The Entrepreneurial Mindset, Harvard Business School Press, Boston, MA.

Miller, D. (1983). "The correlates of entrepreneurship in three types of firms", Management Science, 29: 770-791.

Miles, M.P. (2005). "Entrepreneurial intensity", in Hitt, M.A. & Ireland, R.D. Entrepreneurship, The Blackwell Encyclopedia of Management, Blackwell, London, pp. 91-95.

Miles, M.P. & Arnold, D.R. (1991). "The relationship between marketing orientation and entrepreneurial orientation", Entrepreneurship: Theory and practice, 15, 4: 49-65.

Morris, M.H. (1998). Entrepreneurial Intensity, Quorum Books, Westpoint, CT.

Morris, M.H.; Davis, D. & Allen, J. (1994). "Fostering corporate entrepreneurship: Cross cultural comparison of the importance of individualism versus collectivism", Journal of International Business Studies, 25, 1: 65-89.

Morris, M.H. & Jones, F. (1993). "Human resource

management practices and corporate entrepreneurship", International Journal of Human Resources management, 4, 4: 873-896.

Morris, M.H. & Kuratko, D.F. (2002). Corporate Entrepreneurship, Thomson, New York.

North, D.C. (1968). "Sources of productivity change in ocean shipping 1600-1850", Journal of Political Economy, 76: 953-970.

North, D.C. (1981). Structure and Change in Economic History, Norton, New York.

North, D.C. (1990). Institutions, Institutional Change and Economic Performance, Cambridge University Press, Cambridge.

North, D. (1993). Nobelforedraget: http://www.nobelprize.org/nobel_prizes/economics/laureates/1993/north-lecture.html#not2, date of reading: 4 May 2012.

North, D.C. (1994). "Economic performance through time", American Economic Review, 84: 359-368.

North, D.C. (1996). "Epilogue: Economic performance through time"; in Alston, L.J.; Eggertson, T. & North, D.C. Empirical Studies in Institutional Change, Cambridge University Press, Cambridge (pp.342-355).

North, D.C. (1997). Prologue, 3-13 in J.N. Drobak & J.V.C. Nye, The Frontiers of the New Institutional Economics, Academic

Press, New York.

Pinchot, G. III. (1985). Intrapreneurship: Why you Don't Have to Leave the Corporation to Become an Entrepreneur, Harper & Row, New York.

Polanyi, M. (2009). The Tacit Dimension, University of Chicago Press.

Porter, M.E. (1980). Competitive Strategy, The Free Press, New York.

Porter, M.E. (1985). Competitive Advantage, The Free Press, New York.

Porter, M. E. (1990). The Competitive Advantage of Nations, The Free Press, New York.

Porter, M.E. (1996). "What is strategy", Harvard Business Review, 74/Nov. Dec.

Porter, M. E. (2004). Chapters 2, 3, 4, 5 and 6 in Weller, C.D. Unique Value: Competition Based on Innovation Creating Unique Value, Innovation Press, LLC Publisher, Ashland OH. (pp. 25-187).

Prahalad, C.K. & Bettis, R.A. (1986). "The dominant logic: A new linkage between diversity and performance", Strategic Management Journal, 7: 485-501.

Raiffa, H.C. (1968). Decision Analysis, Addison Wesley,

Reading, MA.

Schollhammer, H. (1982). "Internal corporate entrepreneurship", in Kent, C.A.; Sexton, D.L. & Vesper, K.H. (Ed.). Encyclopedia of Entrepreneurship, Prentice Hall, Englewood Cliffs. pp. 209-229.

Schoemaker, P.J.H. (2002). Profiting from Uncertainty: Strategies for Succeding No Matter what the Future Brings, Free Press, New York.

Schumpeter, J.A. (1934). The Theory of Economic Development, Harvard University Press, Cambridge, MA.

Schumpeter, J.A. (1942). Capitalism, Socialism and Democracy, Harper & Row, New York.

Shane, S. & Venkataraman, S. (2000). "The promise of entrepreneurship as a field of research", Academy of Management Review, 25: 217-226.

Sharma, P. & Chrisman, J.J. (1999). "Toward a reconcilation of the definitional issues in the field of corporate entrepreneurship", Entrepreneurship, Theory and Practice, 23, 3: 11-27.

Stabell, C.D. & Fjellstad, Ø. (1998). "Configuring value for competitive advantage: on chains, shops, and networks, Strategic Management Review, 19, 5: 413-437.

Sterman, J.D. (2000). Business Dynamics: System Thinking and

Modeling for a Complex World, McGraw-Hill, New York.

Tidd, J. (2012). From Knowledge Management to Strategic Competence: Assessing Technological, Market and Organizational Innovation, Imperial College Press, London.

Toffler, A. (1980). The Third Wave, William Morrow, New York.

Utterback, J.M. (1994). Mastering the Dynamics of Innovation; Harvard Business School Press, Boston.

Van der heijden, K. (1996). Scenarios: The Art of Strategic Conversation, Wiley, New York.

Venkataraman, S.; MacMillan, I.C. & McGrath, R.C. (1992). "Progress in research on corporate venturing", in Sexton, D.L. & Kasarda, J.D. (Ed.). The State of the Art of Entrepreneurship: An Exploratory Study, Journal of Business Venturing, 6: 259-285.

Venkataraman, S. & Sarasvathy, S.D. (2001). "Strategy and entrepreneurship: Outlines of an untold story", in Hitt, M.A.; Freeman, R.E. & Harrison, J.S. (Ed.). Handbook of Strategic Management, Blackwell, Oxford, pp. 650-668.

Werther, W.B. & D.B. Chandler (2010). Strategic Corporate Social Responsibility, Sage, London.

Westhead, P.; Wright, M. & Martin, F. (2003). "Habitual entrepreneurs in Scotland: Characteristic search processes, learning and performance". Summary Report, Scotish Enterprise, Glascow.

Zahra, S.A. (1995). "Predictors and financial outcomes of corporate entrepreneurship: An exploratory study", Journal of Business venturing, 6: 259- 285.

Zahra, S.A. & Covin, J.G. (1995). "Contextual influences on the corporate entrepreneurship performance relationship: A longitudinal analysis", Journal of Business venturing, 10, 1: 43-58.

Zahra, S.A.; Jennings, D. & Kuratho, D. (1999). "The antecedents and consequences of firm level entrepreneurship: The state of the field", Entrepreneurship, Theory and Practice, 24: 45-65.

Chapter 2 Managing knowledge resources

Introduction

How knowledge resources can influence organizational

performance, for instance innovation, is demanded from among others Minbaeva (2013:378).

Knowledge is often divided into two main categories: explicit (codifiable) and tacit knowledge (Collins, 2010). Explicit knowledge can be relatively easily formulated using words, figures and symbols, and it can be digitized (Nagy, 2010). This type of knowledge can also be relatively easily communicated to others using ICT. Tacit knowledge is rooted in action (practice) and is related to specific contexts (Polanyi, 2009). It is difficult to communicate this type of knowledge to others in the form of information, because it is difficult to codify or digitize. Tacit knowledge is often an organization's most important strategic resource, because it is difficult for others to acquire and use it, and because it is rooted in the specific problems an organization has to solve. Tacit knowledge can thus be described as an important strategic capability of organizations (Hamel & Prahalad, 1996; 2010). In addition to these two types of knowledge, two other types are also important: hidden knowledge (Kirzner, 1973, 1982; Grant, 2003) and implicit knowledge (see Biack, 2005).

Hidden knowledge is "what we don't know we don't know", which many claim constitutes the basis for creativity and innovation (Kirzner, 1982: 273). It has also been described as "the management of ignorance", which is "the key issue for companies as it is for society" (Grant, 2003: 222), and has been referred to as "previously unthought-of knowledge" (Thomsen, 1992). Kirzner states explicitly that this type of knowledge provides opportunities for developing something that is creative and new, saying "people do not know what it is that they do not know" (Kirzner, 1982: 273).

Implicit knowledge is the knowledge an organization possesses, and which is spread throughout various departments, but which is not utilized or put into productive practice, because knowledge boundaries prevent integration of what an organization knows. It may also be difficult to integrate this knowledge into the larger social system, because there are academic, social, economic, professional and cultural boundaries that inhibit this. The lack of integration of organizations' stores of implicit knowledge results in organizations being "dumber than they need to be".[2]

This chapter focuses on hidden knowledge and its relationship with HR-practices at the organizational level, i.e. here innovation (Ulrich, et.al., 2012). This chapter asks: **How can organizations develop hidden knowledge?**

First we describe the methodology used. Then we develop three assumptions and five propositions concerning the theory for the development of hidden knowledge.

---

[2] We would like to thank Professor Arnulf Hauan, Nord University Business School, Norway, who coined the frame.

Assumptions

By theory we here mean assumptions and the system of propositions and their supposed consequences (Bunge, 1977; 1985). When assumptions and propositions are developed, the next stage is to develop hypotheses which can be empirically tested. In this chapter we develop system of propositions.

Leaders are not aware of the direction or outcomes of developing hidden knowledge, because this is an unknown magnitude. However, what we do know is that analysis is seldom helpful when developing hidden knowledge, because there is no data or information that can form the basis for this kind of analysis (Kirzner, 1982:273).

We choose to call our preferred method of uncovering and developing hidden knowledge the "Columbus Strategy". The analogy with Columbus seems appropriate here because he "didn't know what he didn't know" when he set out from Europe to discover what he thought was the sea route to India. First, the Columbus Strategy focuses on learning through action, reflecting on action and developing knowledge through action and reflection (Argyris, 1993). A second element of the Strategy – to continue the analogy – is that Columbus was motivated by social response, which we relate here to Asplund's motivation theory (Asplund, 2010). A third element of the Columbus Strategy is that people act in response to the system of rewards in the social system which they are a part of, which we relate here to North's action theory (North, 1968; 1981; 1990; 1993; 1994; 1996; 1997).

Assumption 1: Hidden knowledge constitutes the basis of creativity and innovation.

Consequence: If an organization wishes to develop creativity and innovation, it should first develop hidden knowledge.

Assumption 2: The Columbus Strategy aims at identifying and developing hidden knowledge.

Consequence: If organizations wish to develop hidden knowledge, they should first organize and design an organizational learning system, which focus on learning through action.

Assumption 3: The Columbus Strategy relates to Argyris's reflection through action method, Asplund's motivation theory and North's action theory.

Consequence: If organizations wish to develop hidden knowledge, they must:

   a. Embed learning systems in the organization that ensure reflection through action.
   b. Facilitate social responses in relation to activities that promote creative thinking.

c. Design a system of rewards within the organization that promotes creative thinking.

When we operate in the domain of hidden knowledge, it is reasonable to assume that it is largely our beliefs and expectations that guide our actions. The Columbus Strategy is a strategy of discovery, because one journeys into the realm of the unknown without any certain knowledge. One is not even aware of which results one wants to achieve. There is no map of the terrain. A "compass" is no help either except for holding a steady course – but a steady course towards what?

Nevertheless, there is still a great deal of planning involved in projects where the result and the targets are unknown, because we know some of the resources we need, and we have some fundamental knowledge. In reality, however, much of the learning will come while we act, because we must constantly reflect on our actions and what we have learned. We will then be able to react on the basis of what the action resulted in. The pattern is thus: Action, reflection, reaction.

In the scope of opportunities, it is assumed that "the new" will emerge, i.e. something which did not exist before it was created. This process is analogous to how an artist works (da Vinci, 2006): the new knowledge that emerges creates unique combinations and new opportunities (reflection), and a new direction is chosen in light of the new combinations that emerge (reaction). The assumption is that hidden knowledge emerges within the scope of opportunities.

The distinction between exploring new knowledge and exploiting existing knowledge (March, 1991) is not relevant with regard to the domain of hidden knowledge. This is because we are both exploring new knowledge and exploiting existing knowledge simultaneously – uncovering and creating what we don't know we don't know. The knowledge that the organization, as a unified system, does not even know that it does not know exists as a potential for value creation. This type of knowledge cannot be codified or transferred to others as information. Hidden knowledge must be uncovered and created in relation to a practical context (i.e. in the process of action, reflection, reaction). This is a form of systematic learning through action, constantly changing course on the basis of the social responses that occur (Asplund, 2010).

In the knowledge society, and especially for the HR-department, knowledge becomes more important in relation to value creation (see Mitra & Gupta, 2006;Ulrich, 2013;2013a; Wright & Nishii); consequently, managing knowledge resources becomes critical for any organization, regardless of what it does (Wright, et.al., 2011). Management of knowledge activities within an organization will largely involve developing a culture that promotes the development of the different types of knowledge (Drucker, 2007; Ulrich, et.al; 2008; Ulrich et.al, 2008a). Some knowledge already exists at the level of the individual (tacit and explicit), while other types of knowledge emerge through interaction in workshops and teams (tacit and explicit). Some knowledge is spread throughout the organization (implicit knowledge), and then there is also hidden knowledge, or not even knowing what we don't know. Hidden knowledge belongs to the creative domain, and must consequently be created through "voyages of discovery", not unlike an artist's explorations, as mentioned above. The act of "discovering" that we describe here is related to four areas:

- **Ideas**: The ability to develop an innovative and entrepreneurial mindset. We describe here eight techniques for what we designate "ideas management".
- **Systematic learning** through action: Acting first, and then systematically reflecting on the way forward. We present five methods for systematic learning through action.
- **Uniqueness factor**: "Developing the difference which makes a difference" for the organization. We describe here a method for organizations to develop a crucial uniqueness factor, by focusing on the distinction between value creation activities and non-value creation activities for customers.
- **New framework**: We focus here on needs, basic values and intentions, not just demands, stated values and

behaviour. This is done using the method called idealized system design.

Tacit, explicit and implicit knowledge can be mobilized, integrated and coordinated to promote value creation (Ulrich & Smallwood, 2006; 2007). Hidden knowledge, however, must be discovered, identified or created before it can be mobilized, integrated and coordinated. The framework for the Columbus Strategy is shown in Figure 1. The chapter will elaborate on each of the elements of the Columbus Strategy as shown below.

Figure 1: Framework for the Columbus Strategy

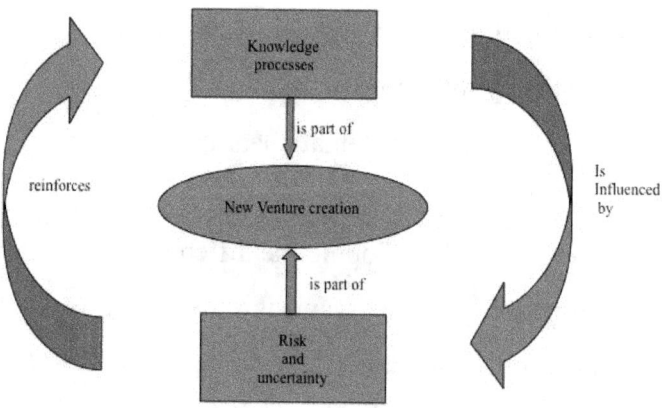

Framework for the Columbus Strategy

Ideas

The ability to develop ideas is important, amongst other things, because organizations are constantly competing to create new business models, new production processes, new products, new services and other types of innovations(Lengnick-Hall & Lengnick-Hall, 2003). New business models, can, for instance, be discovered by benchmarking, but only to a limited extent, because global competition quickly eliminates innovation based on imitation. New business models must therefore be created by individual organizations, based on knowledge that is not so readily copied. This applies both to tacit and hidden knowledge, because these two types of knowledge are not as readily copied as explicit knowledge.

Hidden and tacit knowledge are difficult to imitate, so utilizing these types of knowledge will increase an organization's competitive position. If organizations focus on competitive advantages along the axes of tacit and hidden knowledge, and productivity, and to a lesser extent along the cost parameters in the global knowledge economy, this will improve their competitive position. This is because high-cost countries will never be able to compete on cost with low-cost countries such as China and India in the foreseeable future (Sirmon, et.al., 2007).

Proposition 1: Hidden knowledge is developed through idea management.

Consequence: According to Hammels innovation law (Hamel, 2012), only 1-2 percent of ideas become innovations, so it is necessary to manage idea-generation, idea-selection and the nurturing of selected ideas. It is a myth that innovation comes as a result of spin-of projects; it happens, but most innovation comes from structured processes.

Creative thinking is here understood as being synonymous with what McGrath & MacMillan (2000) call "the entrepreneurial mindset".

Ideas in our context are assumed to develop from creative thinking in an organization. How the creative leader organizes and leads this process is essential for uncovering hidden knowledge. Of course, the first thing that springs to mind in this context is that it is not possible to organize and lead something that one does not know exists! However, it is not the hidden knowledge that should be organized and managed, but rather the process of creating new ideas, which can lead to discovering hidden knowledge. This is analogous to the process tacit knowing which leads to tacit knowledge (Polanyi, 2009).

Some questions of practical relevance can help an organization to find out whether it has the necessary tools to discover and develop hidden knowledge (Johannessen et al., 1993; 1993a):

1. Has the organization established procedures to deal with ideas that spontaneously arise in the organization?
2. Do individuals who contribute ideas receive feedback?
3. Is the management committed to providing a reasoned response concerning rejected ideas within a certain time limit?
4. How is the ideas process organized within the organization?

These are key questions concerning the procedures used for identifying and developing hidden knowledge. The usual answers that are given when organizations are asked such questions are either related to the formal decision-making process in an organization, or are answers of the type: "--- we had some sort of program, --- I am not sure whatever became of it" (Tucker, 2002: 79).

If the process of developing ideas is not organized and managed, given the same status as core business processes, and consequently not emphasized, the organization will lose access to value creation potential. Idea management should be the company's "eye toward the future" (Beer, 1994, Ackoff, 1999; Miller, 1978); it should bring to light ideas that already exist in the organization, connect these together into an integrated whole, and create new business opportunities based on them. This should or could be the main focus of the HR-department of the future (Ulrich, 2013; Wright & Nishii, 2013; Wright & Snell, 1998;Wright et. Al, 2001;Wright &

Younger, 2013).

The purpose of idea management is to make innovation a core process in an organization, because without innovation most organizations will not survive in the global knowledge economy (see Cairncross, 2002: 23Ulrich, 2013a). Tucker (2002: 80-96) describes eight different models for idea management, which in our view can all be used as aspects to uncover hidden knowledge.

The suggestion box

The well-known and proven suggestion box is perhaps past its prime in most organizations. One of the reasons that the suggestion box does not work as intended is that feedback is often poor, and management often has no obligation to provide feedback to individuals in an organization who propose ideas. An improvement on the traditional suggestion box is to commit management to providing reasons for any rejections of ideas within a given time, for instance within a fortnight (see Johannessen et al., 1993; 1993a).

Continuous improvements

Continuous improvements have, as a rule, two focus areas: cost savings and quality improvements. Japanese companies have carried out many such programmes and call them Kaizen. Toyota is a good example of how Kaizen has been particularly successful (see Liker, 2008).

The open-door model

This model allows those who have ideas to go beyond bureaucratic processes and discuss ideas directly with the relevant manager. It is used in many organizations to "open doors" to information and communication channels. For instance, Disney uses this model in an interesting way: three times a year, individuals with ideas have an opportunity to "sell their ideas" directly to the top management (see Tucker, 2002: 89).

Team for new business ideas

This model focuses on launching and obtaining funding for unconventional new products, services or facilities. In practice, such teams work independently of functional areas in an organization. When new ideas are developed, they are analyzed for future potential, and then sold to the management (Kahan, 2013; Unterberg, 2013).

Incubator model

This model has gained recognition in universities and research centres that seek to foster new enterprises based on the knowledge that exists and develops in these environments. The incubator model became popular in the 1990s as a result of the dot-com boom. There are also many examples where this model has been successful, such as Xerox's PARC (Palo Alto Research Center). The PC mouse, for instance, is a result of PARC's activities. Paradoxically for Xerox, it was other organizations that profited from ideas developed at PARC. If organizations are to use this model, then the experience of Xerox should be taken into consideration, so that it is the parent company that profits when new businesses are started up. If not, it is reasonable to assume that those who invest resources in incubator environments will lose interest.

Democracy model

Often we see that idea development is something that is left to senior management and the various forums they participate in. The democracy model is based on ideas that are evenly dispersed throughout an organization, and not reserved for management at various levels.

There are many different types of democracy models. The most extreme type is the one that allows the person with the idea to present it to all the employees, or everyone in his/her department.

The ideas with the most votes will then go on to the next screening level. Another variation of the democracy model is where representatives of the department or the entire organization make up a team that evaluates the ideas that are presented to them.

Innovation team

This model requires an organization "to set up a company-wide network of people with demonstrated skills in innovation and give them very clear marching orders: Go out and find some new ideas that have promise" (Tucker, 2002: 93). However, this model excludes people who lack specialised innovation knowledge, but who could contribute that little extra that was needed to create something new; research shows that using experts and novices together often provides the best solutions (Surowiecki, 2005).

Innovation catalysis

This model uses the same reasoning as in the incubator models with a significant exception – the ideas do not leave the organization. The ideas are tested in each department of the organization, and then are either shelved or proceed to the next step in the evolutionary process.

There are many other models that may prove useful in the idea management process, such as action models, expert-novice models, committed-feedback models, cross-functional teams, etc. The point is that an organization should be conscious of the idea development process, so that ideas are systematized and structured in an appropriate manner, and new knowledge may be developed.

Proposition 2: Idea management is a necessary but not sufficient condition for the development of hidden knowledge. The sufficient condition is that people with ideas in an organization are given an adequate social response. If social feedback does not exist, it will be difficult to develop and uncover the hidden knowledge in an organization.

Consequence: If organizations implement various models of idea management, they have developed a system to enable the fostering of new ideas. These systems however have to be based on a leadership philosophy where the management is obliged to give rationale explanations within a decided timeframe for the neglect of the use of the idea.

Systematic learning through action

This section will show how to use learning through action in a systematic and structured way (Broshyk & Dilworth, 2010) in order to get to grips with hidden knowledge.

We will briefly describe five methods that support learning through action in order to uncover hidden knowledge. These methods are: the falsification method; the input method; "the art of stumbling" method; the anti-flocking method and the judo method.

Just as Columbus could measure progress by navigating by the stars, it is important when learning through action to find fixed anchor points against which progress can be measured. McGrath & MacMillan (2000: 267) use hypotheses for projects where uncertainty is high and there is little factual information available. Hidden knowledge satisfies these two requirements. However, it is important to find some anchor points so that deviations may be measured, in the same way that Columbus used the stars, even though he did not know where he was, and had no concrete information about where he was going. However, he had a hypothesis, which we now know was not correct. Anchor points act as psychological support to reduce the perceived level of uncertainty.

When facts are sparse and hypotheses are largely tentative, projects will be mainly guided by expectations. Expectations may serve as a future indicator for controlling activities in the here and now, which we also find in positive psychology tools (Lewis, 2015:331-338;KO & Donaldson, 2015).

If one formulates expectations and assumptions into hypotheses one can act on, then these hypotheses can either be disproved or confirmed. In this way, learning will emerge through action. This structured method for measuring progress may be termed **the Falsification Method**.

Another way to measure progress when assumptions are very tentative and there is little factual information is to use input factors as performance indicators. For instance, this may be carried out in relation to the specific use of resources, which can be measured over a certain period of time against results that are achieved. This will provide a sense of progress that can be psychologically important for the parties involved (Joseph, 2015:xi-xiii). This may be called **the Input Method** in systematic learning through action.

Most projects will involve working in teams when solving specific problems. If assumptions are large and the knowledge base is small, it will be possible by trial and error to move forward slowly building up the knowledge base. As the team learns more about the key drivers of the project, team members will also learn more about themselves and the others in the team. This is a slow process whereby one gains an understanding of the other members' unique expertise (Bouskila-Yam & Kluger, 2011).

Unexpected findings, side effects and "spin-offs" may be just as important results as whatever you set out to develop in the first place. This may be described as "the Art of Stumbling". For instance, some of the world's greatest things have come about "by chance". Scientists and others often start out by investigating one thing, and then discovering something completely new and different. Electro-magnetism (1820) was discovered in this way, as well as dynamite (1866), acetanilide (1886) – a fever-reducing agent – X-rays (1895), cornflakes (1898), penicillin (1928), antabus (1945), post-it notes (1974), Viagra (1991), the American continent by Columbus (1492), and much more. Learning how to check for side effects and spinoffs requires an essential expertise in order to discover and develop what we don't know we don't know. The progress of the project can then be measured by the success of the side effects and spinoffs, and not necessarily in relation to whether the main objective of the project was reached. However, generally only a prepared mind can exploit such unforeseen events, coincidences and "spin-offs" (Porras, et al. 2008:163-165;Buckingham & Coffman, 2001). This procedure is referred to here as the **Art of Stumbling Method** in relation to systematic learning through action.

When there is a great deal of turbulence in the business world, and uncertainty and complexity are great, it is important, without exception, to focus and simplify. A measure of success when using the Columbus Strategy will be the degree of simplification in what one intends to communicate. Any type of communication, expertise or actions is based on complex underlying structures. To use an analogy, it is not necessary to know how the processes in the brain work, how the nerves operate in the arm, or how the muscle fibres function, when one reaches out to greet a person in a meeting and say "how are you?". Similarly, one does not need to know about the fundamental drivers of a Columbus project. It is often enough to know that any discovery may be useful in some context, although it may be used in useless and destructive ways by others. This requires simplifying what one wishes to communicate, so everyone is able to relate to it at their respective levels.

Complex knowledge structures may also be simplified into a coherent pattern. For instance, although the market may be stable for a period of time, a situation will often develop whereby some actors start to take high risks – the system seems to have omnipotence attributed to it. This results in the market becoming unstable and difficult to predict, and sooner or later the instability will be perceived as chaotic. To protect themselves in this chaos most will follow the "lead sheep", and so a "bubble" develops in the market (Shiller, 2005). Of course, at the end of the chaos the bubble will burst (or result in a "crash landing"). After this, people will be involved in the process of reconstruction, in which a few informed individuals lead in order to build up the market and surrounding social structures again.

What the development of bubbles may be understood as a type of social flocking process, analogous to the behaviour of a flock of birds. In a flock of birds in flight each bird will try to match the direction of the birds around it that it can detect. When the bubble bursts in the market, "the flock" becomes a collection of autonomous individuals. The flocking behaviour after the chaos will slowly but surely lead to a re-stabilization of the market and surrounding social structures; the results are often creatively better than before the chaos. This line of reasoning is related to Schumpeter's concept of creative destruction (see Jonscher, 1999).

It seems reasonable to assume that the six elements in the pattern – stability, omnipotence, instability, flocking (bubble), chaos (crash landing) and new-flocking behaviour – repeat themselves throughout history. If this is correct, then the whole pattern is dynamic. This means that each of the variables will occur in all social systems at different levels and with variable force and effect.

Concerning the development of knowledge in the Columbus Strategy it is important to be aware of where one is located within the pattern, and have an idea about when the next element will occur, assuming that one's insight is correct. From a knowledge perspective, the main insight is to act differently than the others do, because you will then be able to profit where others will not. The implication for action in what we choose to call the **Anti-flocking Method** is to know where you are, and to act differently from the majority. It is under these conditions that hidden knowledge may emerge.

Being different is the difference that really makes a difference, if we are to move into the unknown, if the goal is to discover what others are unable to. This method may be called **the Judo Method**. Always looking to see what others are doing, learning from them and then acting distinctly different from how they act is the core of this process, not unlike the Anti-Flocking Method. However, the Judo Method (Yaffi & Kwah, 2001) differs from the Anti-Flocking Method in that Judo Method makes use of others' skills and expertise. In the Judo Method new phenomena develop as a result of a dialectical process.

The underlying techniques in the Judo Method are as follows (Yaffi & Kwah, 2001: 4-15):

- Not to use force against the other's strength
- To move away from the other
- To block in order to find intervention points
- Intervention points always occur within the other's area, in relation to his/her resources, partners, suppliers or competitors

Proposition 3: Hidden knowledge is developed through an organization's conscious relation to systematic learning through action.

Consequence: If companies implement various methods for systematic learning through action, they will be able to cultivate emerging ideas and spin-offs.

Uniqueness factors

Porras, et al., (2008) provides a perspective that can constitute a basis for discussing what it means to be unique. Imagine that you are wholly concerned with developing the perfect products and services, and you do so with passion, perseverance and dedication. This will be experienced by customers, users, etc. as something positive, whatever the outcome, because they will feel that the organization in question has their needs, wishes and preferences in mind (Brown & Ryan, 2015). To strive for perfection as Porras et al. express means to be constantly looking for opportunities to uncover hidden knowledge, so that new products and services can be provided to customers, users, etc.

However, the catch with continually striving for "the perfect" is that customers are often more interested in something that works and satisfies than in something perfect (Simon, 1997). If the perfect creates no significant added value for the customer, and is also more expensive, then it is reasonable to assume that the customer will not be interested. The question is always whether the organization in question is able to stand out in areas which the customer perceives as representing added value. We call this the uniqueness factor. In other words, in relation to the view of Porras et al., developing hidden knowledge is not necessarily useful to the customer if it does not result in added value.

The uniqueness factor says something about what makes a service or product unique in relation to what competitors are able to deliver. It is an objective element in the sense that customers are tested for perceptions in areas that lead to added value. In other words, the uniqueness factor addresses whether or not there is added value for customers, while a "perfect" product does not necessarily provide any added value for customers.

Tests to detect any uniqueness factor are twofold and relatively simple. First, it is important to identify what is important to customers related to what the organization delivers. Then the deliverable's uniqueness is tested in relation to others that provide the same service or product, in those areas which are most likely to result in added value for the customer; in this context, it is important to have a high degree of uniqueness, i.e. a difference that makes a difference (Bateson, 1972:271-272).

An easy way to get to grips with hidden knowledge related to the uniqueness factor may be to consider what is described as NVA (non valued-added) (Liker, 2008). By focusing on NVA, and then eliminating all activities that do not result in added value for customers, the uniqueness factor will increase.

Creating added value for customers is objective in the sense that it can be tested by analyzing the customer experience. It is the individual experience where the customer participates in determining NVA, thereby creating the pre-condition for developing new products and services.

VA (value added for customers) and NVA (non value added) can be specifically examined along three dimensions with specified variables; this is similar to LaSalle & Britton (2003: 13). For each of the variables in Figure 4, two questions are asked:

1. How can VA be promoted?

2. What can be done to remove NVA?

By asking these two questions of the variables in Figure 2, hidden knowledge may be discovered, uncovering what we don't know we don't know.

Figure 2: Domains and variables[3] for VA and NVA aimed at uncovering hidden knowledge

---

[3] These domains and variables are adapted from LaSalle & Britton (2003: 13).

Domains / Variables	Emotional	Intellectual	Creative
	1. Well-being 2. Personal growth 3. Caring 4. Relationships 5. Status 6. Self-esteem 7. Belonging 8. Identity	1. Learning 2. Knowledge 3. Control 4. Quality 5. Reliability 6. Consistency 7. Precision 8. Efficiency	1. Excitement 2. Freedom 3. Confidence 4. Integrity 5. Chaos 6. Ideas 7. Aesthetic 8. Presentation

If the variables are used in a workshop focusing on determining NVA, this may be calculated by systematically reviewing the variables in the three domains, or as a result of considering the relationships between the variables in the different domains; the latter method results in 552 combinations (n (n-1)).

The first step in discovering hidden knowledge, using Figure 4 and the two questions related to the variables, is to consider the answers to the questions. The second step is to evaluate the importance of NVA and VA in relation to what emerged in the first step. The third step is to select the hidden knowledge that creates the greatest uniqueness factor for the organization. The fourth step is to integrate the selected hidden knowledge in the business model. The fifth and final step is to create added value for the customer in relation to the hidden knowledge selected.

Proposition 4: Hidden knowledge is developed when using value added (VA) and non value added (NVA) questions, in relation to the domains and variables in figure 4.

Consequence: If an organization wishes to increase its degree of uniqueness, it should eliminate all activities that do not create added value for customers (NVA).

New frameworks

In cases of emerging events, which may be coincidences or something occurring by pure chance, one way to interpret and understand them is to frame the organization's activities in a new way. For instance, we can frame arbitrary events in a market so that we understand them as a sub-segment of the market. For example, a "housing bubble" may be framed in such a way that it only applies to the housing market. A "tulip bubble" (Dash, 2010) may be framed so that it only applies to investments in tulips. An "IT bubble" may be framed so that it only applies to investments in IT companies' stocks, etc.

It will be possible to envision new and emerging skills as constituting a future core competence. For instance, cultural resources may be framed so that certain norms and values are valid while others are not. We will also be able to frame our understanding of leadership, in order to focus on specific competencies which a leader in the knowledge society should have (Bolman, 2013). The purpose of using a new framework is to give meaning and legitimacy to a change of course, Normann argues (2001).

One framework that has proved useful in several contexts is framing a potential market in terms of the customer's needs, rather than customer demands. For example, Amazon.com uses such a strategy: by analyzing customer demand – a customer's purchasing history – Amazon establishes a customer profile which is used to predict the customer's needs with an eye to stimulating the customer's future purchases, offering the customer specific products on the basis of his/her past purchasing profile.

People's actions may also be framed in relation to intent and behaviour. In psychology, action is often defined as intention plus behaviour. What we often do in practice is to interpret people by their behaviour. However, if we frame in an understanding of the customer in relation to intention rather than just his/her behaviour, then other possibilities may emerge. The new elements that emerge may be used as intervention points in analyzing his/her needs, wants and preferences.

By framing customers in relation to the needs they express, their basic values and their intentions, then it is possible to get to grips with hidden knowledge concerning the customer, which can help an organization to re-design and re-define both its business model and market.

Using a new framework is appropriate when an organization is at a "point of no return" and incremental improvements will not lead to future success. In such a situation, it is reasonable to assume that it will be breakthrough strategies that promote success.

In order to get to grips with hidden knowledge in the context of a new framework, idealized design (see Ackoff et al., 2006) is a conceptual tool that may help to uncover what we don't know we don't know.

Idealized design can quite simply be defined as imagining how the future ideal solution would have been today, and then mentally working your way backwards to the point where you actually are today. This is what Karl Weick calls "Future Perfect Thinking" (Weick, 1979). The point of focusing on what the ideal solution would have been today and not, say, in five years, is that: "…we know that where we say today we would like to be five years from now, is not where we will want to be when we get there. Thing will happen between now and then that will affect our goals and objectives. By focusing on what we want right now, we can eliminate that potential source of error" (Ackoff, et al., 2006: xxxvi).

Idealized design as a method may be formulated as a stepwise process (Ackoff, et al., 2006: 5-25). First you define the problem-complex the organization finds itself in. Then you imagine what the ideal situation would have been in the present. Then one realizes the desired present situation, by uncovering which resources that would have had to exist in the present, in order for the ideal situation to manifest itself.

In idealized design schemes, then, ideally all affected persons should participate in the development process, because this increases the range of ideas that can be explored in relation to discovering and developing hidden knowledge in an organization. The duration of such an idealized design process will be over five to six days, says Ackoff, et al. (2006:31). There are three rules that the process should bear in mind (Ackoff, et.al.,: 33-36):

1. A burning desire should resonate in the process, not just decisions based on existing resources.

2. All stakeholders should be brought into the process.

3. Only positive contributions should be accepted; critics and realists must limit their enthusiasm.

Proposition 5: Idealized design is an effective method for developing hidden knowledge.

Consequence: If an organization chooses idealized design in order to develop hidden knowledge, it must follow the processes and guidelines this method is subject to.

Theoretical policy implications – Knowledging

Nonaka & Takeuchi (1995) and Nonaka and Kono (1998) have developed the SECI model (socialization, externalization, combination and internalization). This model is mainly oriented towards epistemology. Hidden knowledge relates to the intellectual, emotional and creative domains, and is therefore located between epistemology and ontology.

The epistemological dimension includes and distinguishes between tacit knowledge, explicit knowledge and implicit knowledge. The ontological dimension is here understood as hidden knowledge, because this knowledge that has not yet become a part of our consciousness; it has not yet become part of our epistemology, but is part of the ontological dimension, even if we don't know where to look for it. We believe that knowledge can be developed by individuals, teams and organizations. Individuals develop and transfer tacit knowledge and explicit knowledge (Grant, 2003). Teams develop and communicate implicit and hidden knowledge. Organizations mobilize, coordinate and integrate hidden, tacit, implicit and explicit knowledge. Several authors have discussed the knowledge process by distinguishing between levels –

individuals, teams and organizations – as well as making distinctions between epistemology and ontology (see Hedlund, 1994; Nonaka & Takeuchi, 1995; Zollo & Winter, 2002; Nonaka & Konno, 1998).

We use the term "knowledging" to describe the, connection between epistemology and ontology at the individual, team and organizational levels. If knowledge creation is a learning process, we can distinguish four processes each operating on three levels (individual, team, organization) that use the four knowledge domains (tacit, explicit, implicit and hidden). The four processes are knowledge development, mobilization, integration and coordination (Sanchez, 2001). We illustrate the various processes in Figure 5. For pedagogical reasons, we have not included the processes that run between levels, nor have we considered the knowledging that occurs between the organization and the external world, so as not to further complicate the processes. Figure 3 should therefore be understood as a descriptive model of knowledging.

Figure 3: Knowledging at the individual, team and organizational levels

Knowledge types \ Knowledging	Development of knowledge	Mobilization of knowledge	Integration of knowledge	Coordination of knowledge
Tacit knowledge	Practical contexts	Mentoring	Master-apprentice relationships	Organization
Explicit knowledge	Systematic cognitive processes	Clear intentions	Experience transference	Results focus
Implicit knowledge	Structural relations	Networks	Multi-disciplinary teams	Clear aims
Hidden knowledge	Columbus strategies	Innovation processes	Entrepreneurship	Incentives

Conclusion

The research question was: How can organizations develop hidden knowledge?

The mini theory consisting of three assumptions and five propositions that has been developed is the answer of the research question.

Bibliography

Ackoff, R.L. (1999). Recreating the Corporation, OUP, New York.

Ackoff, R.L.; Magidson, J. & Addison, H.J. (2006). Idealized Design, Wharton School Publishing, New Jersey, Pennsylvania.

Argyris, C. (1993). Knowledge for Action, Jossey Bass, San Francisco.

Asplund, (2010). Det sosiale livets elementære former, Korpen, Stockholm.

Bateson, G. (1972). Steps to an ecology of mind, Ballantine Books, New York.

Beer, S. (1994). Diagnosing the System for Organizations, John Willey & Sons, New York.

Bicak, K. (2005). International Knowledge Transfer Management, Shaker Verlag, Aachen.

Bolman, L.G. (2013). Reframing Leadership, The Leaders Guide to the Four Dimensions of Organizational Life, Jossey Bass, London.

Bouskila-Yam, O. & Kluger, A.N. (2011). Strength based performance appraisal and goal setting, Human Resources Management Review, 21:137-147.

Broshyk, Y. & Dilworth, R. (2010). Action Learning: History and Evolution, Palgrave Macmillan, London.

Brown, K.W. & Ryan, R.M. (2015). A Self-determination theory perspective on forstering healthy self-regulation from within and without, i Joseph, S. (Ed.). Positive Psychology in Practice, Wiley, New York. S. 139-159.

Buckingham, M. & Coffman, C. (2001). First break all the rules, Simon & Schuster, London.

Bunge, M. (1977). Treatise on basic philosophy. Vol. 3. Ontology I: The furniture of the world. Dordrecht, Holland: D. Reidel.

Bunge, M. (1985). Philosophy of Science and Technology, Part I, Reidel, Dordrecht.

Bunge, M. (1998). Social Science under Debate: A Philosophical Perspective, University of Toronto Press, Toronto.

Cairncross, F. (2002). The Company of the Future, Harvard Business School Press, Boston.

Collins, H. (2010). Tacit and Explicit knowledge, University of Chicago Press, Chicago.

Dash, M. (2010). Tulipomania, Phoenix, London.

da Vinci, L. (2006). Leonardo da Vinci: The Complete Works, David & Charles, New York.

Drucker, P.F. (2007). Management Challenges for the 21st century, Butterworth-Heinemann, New York.

Hedlund, G. (1994). "A model of knowledge management and the N-form corporation", Strategic Management Journal, 15: 73-91.

Grant, R.M. (2003). "The knowledge-based view of the firm", in Faulkner, D.O. & Campell, A. The Oxford Handbook of Strategy, Oxford University Press, Oxford (pp. 203-231).

Hamel, G. (2012). What matters now: How to Win in a World of Relentless Change, Ferocious Competition, and Unstoppable Innovation, John Wiley & Sons, New York

Hamel, G. & Prahalad, C.K. (1996). Competing for the Future, Harvard Business School Press, Boston.

Hamel, G. & Prahalad, C.K. (2010). Strategic Intent, Harvard Business School Press, Boston.

Johannessen, J-A & Olaisen, J. (1993). "The information intensive organization: A study of governance, control and communication in a Norwegian shipyard", in International Journal of Information Management (13) 5: 341-354.

Johannessen, J-A., Olaisen, J. & Hauan, A (1993a). "The challenge of innovation in a Norwegian shipyard: facing the Russian market", in the European Journal of Marketing, 27, 3 :23-

39.

Jonscher, C. (1999). The Evolution of Wired Life, John Wiley, New York.

Joseph, S. (2015). Forword, i Joseph, S. (Ed.). Positive Psychology in Practice, Wiley, New York. S. Xi-xiii.

Kahan, S. (2013). Getting Innovation Right: How to Turn Ideas into Outcomes, Jossey Bass, London.

Kirzner, I. (1973). Competition and Entrepreneurship, University of Chicago Press, Chicago.

Kirzner, S. (1982). "The theory of entrepreneurship in economic growth"; in Kent, C.A.; Sexton, D. L. & Vesper, K.H. (Ed.). Encyclopedia of Entrepreneurship, Prentice Hall, Englewood Cliffs. N.J.

Ko, I. & Donaldson, S.I. (2011). Applied positive organizational psychology: The state of science and practice, i Donaldson, S.I.; Csikszentmihalyi,M. & Nakamura, J. (Eds.). Applied positive psychology, Routledge, New York, s. 137-154.

LaSalle, D. & Britton, T.A. (2003). Priceless: Turning Ordinary Products into Extraordinary Experiences, Harvard Business School Press, Boston.

Lengnick-Hall, M.L. & Lengnick-Hall, C.A. (2003). Human Resource Management in the Knowledge Economy, BK, San

Francisco.

Lewis, S. (2015). Bringing Positive Psychology to Organizational Psychology, i Joseph, S. (Ed.) Positive Psychology in Practice, Wiley, New York.

Liker, J. (2008). Toyota Culture: The Heart and Soul of the Toyota Way, McGraw Hill, New York.

March, J.G. (1991). "Exploration and exploitation in organizational learning", Organizational Science, 2: 71-87.

McGrath, R. & MacMillan, I. (2000). The Entrepreneurial Mindset, Harvard Business School Press, Boston, MA.

Miller, J.G. (1978). Living Systems, McGaw-Hill, New York.

Minbaeva, D.(2013). Strategic HRM in building microfoundations of organizational knowledgebased performance, Human Resource Management Review, 23:378-390.

Mitra, A. & Gupta, A. (2006). Creating Agile Business Systems with Reusable Knowledge, Cambridge University Press, Cambridge.

Nagy, K.H. (2010). Transforming Government and Building the Information Society, Springer, Berlin.

Nonaka, I. & Konno, N. (1998). "The concept of BA: Building a foundation for knowledge creation", California Management Review, 40, 3: 40-54.

Nonaka, I. & Takeuchi, H. (1995). The Knowledge Creating Company: How Japanese Companies Create the Dynamics of Innovation, Oxford University Press, Oxford.

Normann, R. (2001). Reframing Business: When the Map Changes the Landscape, John Wiley & Sons, London.

North, D.C. (1968). "Sources of productivity change in ocean shipping 1600-1850", Journal of Political Economy, 76: 953-970.

North, D.C. (1981). Structure and Change in Economic History, Norton, New York.

North, D.C. (1990). Institutions, Institutional Change and Economic Performance, Cambridge University Press, Cambridge.

North, D. (1993). Nobelforedraget: http://www.nobelprize.org/nobel_prizes/economics/laureates/1993/north-lecture.html#not2, date of reading: 4 May 2012.

North, D.C. (1994). "Economic performance through time", American Economic Review, 84: 359-368.

North, D.C. (1996). "Epilogue: Economic performance through time"; in Alston, L.J.; Eggertson, T. & North, D.C. "Empirical studies in institutional change", Cambridge University Press, Cambridge (pp. 342-355).

North, D.C. (1997). Prologue, 3-13 in J.N. Drobak & J.V.C. Nye "The frontiers of the new institutional economics", Academic

Press, New York.

Pfeffer, J. & Sutton, I. (2000). The Knowing-Doing Gap, Harvard Business School Press, Boston.

Polanyi, M. (2009). The Tacit Dimension, University of Chicago Press, Chicago.

Porras, J.; Emery, S. & Thompson, M. (2008). Success Built to Last, Jossey Bass, San Francisco.

Sanchez, R. (2001). Knowledge Management and Organizational Competence, Oxford University Press, Oxford.

Shiller, R.J. (2005). Irrational Exuberance, Princeton University Press, Princeton.

Simon, H. A. (1997). Administrative Behavior: A Study of Decision-making Processes in Administrative Organizations: A Study of Decision-making Processes in Administrative Organisations, The Free Press, London.

Sirmon, D., Hitt, M. & Irelanf, R. (2007). Managing firm resources in dynamic environments to create value: looking inside the black box, Academy of Management Review, 32, 1:273-292.

Surowiecki, J. (2005). The Wisdom of Crowds, Abacus, New York.

Tucker, R.B. (2002). Driving Growth through Innovation: How

Leading Firms are Transforming their Futures, Berrett-Koehler Publisher, San Francisco.

Ulrich, D. (2013). Forword, in Ulrich, D.; Brockbank, W.; Younger, J. & Ulrich, M. (eds.), Global HR Competencies: Mastering Competitive Value from the Outside in, McGraw Hill, New York. S. v-xxi.

Ulrich, D. (2013a). Future of Global HR: What´s Next?, in Ulrich, D.; Brockbank, W.; Younger, J. & Ulrich, M. (eds.), Global HR Competencies: Mastering Competitive Value from the Outside in, McGraw Hill, New York. S. 255-268.

Ulrich, D.; Younger, J.; Brockbank, W. & Ulrich, M. (2012). HR from the Outside in: Six Compeencies for the Future of Human Resources, mcgraw Hill, New York.

Unterberg, B. (2013). Crowdstorm: The Future of Ideas, Innovation, and Problem Solving is Collaboration, John Willey & Sons, London.

Yaffi, D.B. & Kwak, M. (2001). Judo Strategy, Harvard Business School Press, Boston.

Zollo, M. & Winter, S.G. (2002). "Deliberate learning and the evolution of dynamic capabilities", Organization Science, 13: 339-351.

Weick, K.E. (1979). The Social Psychology of Organizing, John

Wiley, London.

Wright, P.M. & Nishii, L.H. (2013). Strategic HRM and Organizational behaviour: Integrating multiple levels of analysis, i Paauwe, J.; Guest, D.E. & Wright, P.M. (2013). HRM & Performance: Achievements & Challenges, Wiley, London. S. 97-110.

Wright, P.M. & Snell, S.A. (1998). Towards a unifying framework for exploring fit and flexibility in strategic human resource management, Academy of Management Review, 23:756-772.

Wright, P.; Dunford, B. & Snell, S. (2001). Human resources and the resource based view of the firm, Journal of Management, 27:701-721.

Wright, P.M.; Boudreau, J.W.; Pace, D.A.; Libby Sartain, E.; McKinnon, P.; Antoine, R.L. (Eds.). (2011). The Chief HR Officer: Defining the New Role of Human Resource Leaders, Jossey-Bass, London.

White, J. & Younger, J. (2013). The Global Perspective, in Ulrich, D.; Brockbank, W.; Younger, J. & Ulrich, M. (eds.); Global HR Competencies: Mastering Competitive Value from the Outside in, McGraw Hill, New York. S. 27-53.

Introduction to innovation Vol. 2

Jon-Arild Johannessen (Ed.)

Chapter 3 Knowledge management and innovation

Introduction

Through the increasing attention directed towards ICT, we have seen a strong emphasis on explicit knowledge, but also an interest in tacit knowledge (Collins, 2010:1-15). This has put tacit knowledge (Polanyi, 1958; 2009) in the forefront of research on organizational learning and innovation (Bush, 2008; Lam, 2000:487-513; Garavan & McGuire, 2015; Donate, et.al., 2015; Mascitelli, 2000).

Information and communications technologies are key to innovation processes in companies today (Johannessen, et.al., 2001; Contini & Lanzara, 2008).

Organizational learning and innovation are dependent on access to knowledge (King, 2009:1-13; Grillitsch & Rekers, 2015). This means knowledge that is external to the business as well as the development of new knowledge within a specific business (Gangi & Wasko, 2009:199-213). The real point, however, is that much of this knowledge is tacit, and tacit knowledge had not received attention from researchers, managers or politicians prior to the 1990s (Nonaka, 1991; 1994; Nonaka & Takeuchi, 1995; Nonaka & Ichijo,1997).

The research question we will be investigating here is: What is the relation between tacit knowledge organizational learning and innovation?

To answer this question we ask three questions:

1. What is tacit knowledge and tacit knowing, and how is it linked to organizational learning?
2. How can tacit knowledge be typologized and linked to different types of organizational learning?
3. How do different types of tacit knowledge and organizational learning affect organizational learning and innovation?

Organizing of the chapter

The chapter is organized around the three research questions. First we describe the method used, conceptual generalization, then we start with research question one.

What is tacit knowledge and tacit knowing and how is it linked to organizational learning?

One starting point for Polanyi (2009:4) is: "...we can know more than we can tell" and, along the same lines, "...nothing that we know can be said precisely" (Polanyi, 1958: 87-88). Accordingly, the basis for Polanyi's concept of tacit knowledge is that we know more than we are able to communicate to others in the form of information. Examples of adequate methods may be mechanisms that release and combine explicit and tacit knowledge. When tacit knowledge is to be transferred from one person to another, this cannot be done completely by means of either language or images (Cannon, 2002). When a master needs to show an apprentice what he/she means, he/she will often point at the object in question, or make the apprentice aware of the significant features of a particular situation. The master may point out signs that the apprentice needs to be aware of to keep the situation under control. For example, there may be particular types of sound that indicate that one process or another is starting to go wrong. This method of defining something by pointing out a particular thing or situation is referred to by Polanyi (2009:6) as ostensive definition. The transmission of tacit knowledge to an apprentice is an active creative process; it is not one of passive transmission from master to apprentice (Polanyi, 2009:6). The process of apprenticeship is dependent in part on the apprentice themselves gradually finding out knowledge that the master is unable to transmit, but which becomes apparent through the situation/context at any particular time (Cannon, 2002). This active process means that the tacit knowledge possessed by the apprentice becomes different to that of the master. The apprentice integrates this tacit knowledge into their existing knowledge-base, and makes it their own. Tacit knowledge will comprise a proportion of the knowledge-base in most occupations. This applies to, for example, nurses, pre-school teachers, teachers, managers, artists, technicians, researchers etc.

This type of knowledge cannot be learned through formalised and codified procedures that are divorced from practice.

The distinction between explicit and tacit knowledge may be understood in relation to *wissen* (German: "knowing what") and *kønnen* ("knowing how"). With regard to the above, the development of tacit knowledge may be said to always consist of three elements: knowing, wanting to know and the practical context.

It is by becoming intimate with phenomena or problems - "dwelling in them" (Polanyi, 2009: 18) - that we can understand their inner meaning. In other words, it is intimacy and extensive experience of a phenomenon in its context that constitutes the approach to tacit knowledge and thereby also a foundation for learning. It is precisely this sensitivity, attained through intimacy by application and execution, that leads to the development and transferral of tacit knowledge. Polanyi (2009: 55) expresses this in the following way: "--- tacit knowing achieves comprehension by indwelling, and that all knowledge consists of or is rooted in such acts of comprehension."

Tacit knowledge exists, says Molander (1993: 40), in "the action and the judgements that are carried out in relation to the action". The word 'and' is crucially important here: the action *and* the judgements. It is not only the action or the judgements by which tacit knowledge may be understood but the reflection that is made before, during and after the action. This links tacit knowledge to the learning process.

There are three main processes connected to tacit knowledge: action, reflection and interaction. The action is crucial to tacit knowledge. It is through the execution of activities that players develop, transfer and integrate tacit knowledge in the social system. However, reflection is also essential if learning is to be achieved. The action is at the core of tacit knowledge, but around this core lie reflection and interaction. The interaction may be divided into two components. Firstly, there is interaction with the object, phenomenon or problem that is to be understood or solved. Secondly, there is interaction between individuals who possess knowledge of the phenomenon, object, etc. The action takes place in the moment of time. However, reflection takes place before, during and after the action. The interaction has the same time dimension as the reflection, i.e. the players interact before, during and after the action. The action, reflection and interaction are connected by the fact that the players participate and contribute in a practical learning context.

As mentioned above, tacit knowledge is developed through familiarity with a phenomenon or object; this is referred to here as the phenomenal structure of tacit knowledge. Tacit knowledge is transferred through interaction between the possessor of tacit knowledge and the individual who wants to learn; this is referred to here as the functional structure of tacit knowledge. The integration of tacit knowledge in a system or between systems is dependent on familiarity with the context in which players are able to act and interact in relation to specific objectives; a process where learning by dialogue is the crucial element (Little, 1995:175-181; Matte & Cooren, 2015). This is referred to here as the contextual structure of tacit knowledge.

The phenomenal, functional and contextual structures of tacit knowledge may be related to Polanyi's later work (2009), where he distinguishes between "phenomenal", "functional" and "semantic" structures of tacit knowledge.

The development, transfer and integration of tacit knowledge require action, reflection and emotional engagement. However, these three elements are only necessary conditions for the processes of this type of knowledge. In addition, the transfer and integration of tacit knowledge require that relations between players are based on trust and a positive, helping attitude; this reinforces confidence in relationships and facilitates the knowledge processes mentioned above (Amirkhani & Heydari, 2015).

Tacit knowledge is developed, transferred and integrated as a type of attention focusing on a phenomenon, function and context; it is the constant focusing over a period of time that develops awareness towards the signals that practice transmits. Polanyi (1958: 61) says "Like the tool, the sign or the symbol can be conceived as such only in the eyes of a person who relies on them to achieve or to signify something. This reliance is a personal commitment which is involved in all acts of intelligence by which we integrate some things subsidiarily to the centre of our focal attention". Tacit knowledge and practice are thus closely related but distinct concepts; it is developed and transferred through learning by doing, learning by using, single loop learning, double loop learning (Schön, 1987; 1988), where there exists a relationship between a master and an apprentice, an expert and a novice or one who knows and one who wants to know. This relationship is based on discipline. By discipline here we mean the word's original meaning: learning from someone who knows.

Skills are developed through repeated practice until they become automatic or part of the skills are considered tacit knowledge; they can then be executed without conscious control of the separate activities, so that the doer can focus attention on a higher level of perfection. Physical activities are assimilated so they become conditioned reflexes when carried out by the expert. However, to reach this level presupposes that the development of the tacit knowledge is learned through "slow repetitive practice to set up conditioned reflex programs in the brain" (Robinson, 1996: 127). For certain motor skills, such as playing the piano, one might say the fingers *are the brain*: that is, the memory of how to play is in the fingertips. Similarly, your fingers can remember how to dial a particular phone number even though you may not be able to verbalise it.

It is important to be aware of the fact that all explicit knowledge presupposes tacit components. Rolf (1995: 63) writes "All knowledge which is not tacit, presupposes tacit knowledge, says Polyani". For Polanyi, the tacit dimension is the result of pre-conceptual actions that are integrated through experience into the context. The tacit dimension represents the practical aspect of a situation.

Tacit knowledge is the practical knowledge used to perform a task, and it is also "the knowledge that is used as a tool to handle what is being focused on" (Sveiby, 1997: 30). Consequently, tacit knowledge in a business context is: practical, action-oriented, experience-based, context-linked and personal, but not subjective or relative.

How can tacit knowledge be typologized and linked to organizational learning?

We will develop a typology of tacit knowledge where each type of tacit knowledge has its own implications with regard to management and innovation processes.

Tacit knowledge is the result of different types of learning processes, which we will denote here using the term "tacit knowledge processes"[4]. Polanyi expresses these processes in the following way: "Tacit knowing is a process of a complex whole, a pattern which escapes when taken apart for analysis. But tacit knowing is not only involved in the process by which tacit knowledge is gained. It is also involved in the processes by which all knowledge is gained" (Polanyi, 1958: 49). For Polanyi, tacit knowledge processes are the dominant principle of all knowledge. Tacit knowledge processes rely on focus and perception of a system of details which we cannot specify or test scientifically. However, this does not apply to tacit knowledge, resulting from tacit knowledge processes. Tacit knowledge is objective in the sense that it may be tested with regard to its consequences, although the tacit knowledge processes may not be tested. The logic of this is as follows: If knowledge has a function, it must also have an effect, and if it has an effect then it must be possible to discover this effect.

A nurse's clinical insight may be said to provide an example of tacit knowledge; the results of this clinical insight may be tested and revealed empirically using quality evaluation. However, the system of elements that constitute clinical insight, i.e. the tacit knowledge processes, are not possible to detect. But there are different types of tacit knowledge; some types of tacit knowledge may be possible to communicate to others as information rules of

---

[4] "Tacit knowledge processes" is here synonymous with Polanyi's "tacit knowing", which denotes the processes leading to tacit knowledge.

thumb and holistic causal understanding (fig. 1), while other types are very difficult to communicate as information (intuition and pattern understanding (fig. 1).

To sum up, some types of tacit knowledge may naturally be transferred to others as information, while other types are not transferable and cannot be stored (for example, electronically). This may have consequences in organisations: for instance, if a hospital has implemented a strategy whereby all knowledge has to be stored on electronic media, this may be very harmful for patients and knowledge development in the institution, because tacit knowledge may be turned down.

Tacit knowledge is essential for success in a number of tasks, skills and professions, such as management, sales, law, software design, medicine, education, music, computing, pottery, wine testing, and in skills related to selecting fish, tea, coffee, olives, chestnuts, etc. (Marchant & Robinson, 1999; Argyris, 1999; Sheng, et.al., 2015; Nishinaka, et.al., 2015).

Furthermore, tacit knowledge is necessary when practicing certain skills such as swimming, cycling and riding. When we speak of someone having a flair for something, a gut feeling, a good nose, an inner voice, or having skills at their fingertips, then this more often than not concerns a type of tacit knowledge. Perhaps another example of tacit knowledge is when we speak of a craftsman who needs to "see" the pattern in the wood when making a Steinway piano. Does the pattern in the wood affect the tone of the piano lid? Analogous to this is the importance of understanding patterns for leaders; such a skill determines the difference between a good leader and an excellent one. The excellent leader is able to use tacit knowledge strategically when he/she gains an overview through the complexity that often characterises today's businesses, or the intuitive leader who "knows" what is about to happen (Donate, et.al, 2015). We denote in fig. 1 that it is intuition and understanding of patterns which allows the excellent leader to grasp what is innovative and what wouldn't have been realized unless he/she had created the conditions to facilitate the practical implementation of an innovation.

In addition to level of competence, tacit knowledge may be divided into two main types: specific and strategic (Wagner, 1987)[5]. Specific tacit knowledge refers to the practical knowledge that is useful when performing a specific task here and now, usually face to face with the another person or in direct interaction with the object/ instrument, etc. Strategic tacit knowledge refers to the practical knowledge that is useful when achieving long-term goals, and being able to relate current tacit knowledge in a future and broader context; hence the term strategic tacit knowledge.

It is reasonable to assume that different tasks in which tacit

---

[5] Wagner uses the terms "local tacit knowledge" and "global tacit knowledge". We choose for reasons of appropriateness to use terms specific and strategic, without diverging from the interpretation of Wagner's concepts.

knowledge is used require degrees of both specific and strategic tacit knowledge (cf. Wagner et al. 1999). We choose two professional levels: expert and competent. We make this distinction deliberately, and thus choose to ignore the five-level classification of novice to expert which Dreyfus and Dreyfus introduced (1986). We choose this dichotomy for simplicity, but also because we are focusing on tacit knowledge, and the novice cannot be said to possess tacit knowledge to any large degree. The novice uses essentially algorithmic rules, instructions, and so on. The competent individual is fully trained and has some experience (5-7 years)(Simon, 1987; Kahneman & Klein, 2009), but still operates at a low level of tacit knowledge, related to the knowledgeable expert with extensive experience (7-11 years)(Klein, 1998; 2003). The competent individual masters the practical aspects in the work that has to be done, but still lacks the grasp on things and situations that the knowledgeable expert has. The expert is considered to be a person with extensive practical experience within his/her field. The expert is one who masters practical aspects and he/she can also explain why his/her actions are important while putting them into a larger context. Using the four concepts of specific tacit knowledge, strategic tacit knowledge, competent, and expert, we have developed a typology of tacit knowledge shown in Figure 1 below.

In the typology we introduce four types of organizational learning: single-loop, double-loop, deutero and paradigmatic learning.

Argyris & Schøn (1978: 26-29) uses three of the learning concepts, but not paradigmatic learning, which here is associated from Bateson (1972: 303)[6]. We have tried to link the four types of tacit knowledge to the four types of organizational learning in order to visualize the connection between tacit knowledge and organizational learning. When we explain the typology we go further in to the links between different types of tacit knowledge and different types of organizational learning.

---

[6] Bateson uses the concept of "calibration". This concept may lead to unwanted associations, therefor we introduce paradigmatic learning as we think cover Batesons concept of calibration

Figure 1. Typology of tacit knowledge linked to organizational learning

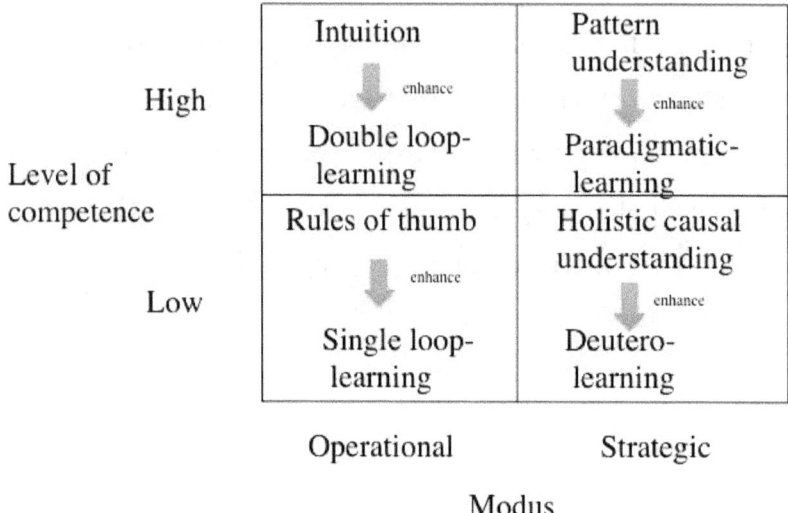

We will elaborate on the different types of tacit knowledge linked to organizational learning in the following section.

Explanation of the different types of tacit knowledge and organizational learning

Rules of thumb and single loop-learning

The development of the use of rules of thumb in relation to the above figure may be said to have the following characteristics (Anzai & Simon, 1979):

* The novice first uses a method based on trial and error, resulting in many errors in relation to a set standard or performance criteria.
* On the basis of these results, which include a number or errors, the novice develops procedures for avoiding the errors, resulting in a more focused approach to problem solving.
* This results in more appropriate action being taken, based on a breakdown of the main target into various objectives.
* By organising the various objectives, a goal-oriented action strategy is developed.
* The new strategy is structured and systematized to develop compact action procedures.

This is in line with single-loop learning. Single loop learning is learning of rigid responses (Bateson, 1972: 284). This means that the same type of action later on will be comprehensed in the same way.

Learning of tricks (Polany, 2009) is an example of single-loop learning, which looks like rules of thumb. Rules of thumb may also be developed through "learning by using" (Rosenberg, 1982).

The novice does not use rules of thumb, but rather rules. When tacit knowledge is developed in a practical context over a period of time, information is organised and structured so that the novice is gradually able to move up to a competent level (5-7 years) (Simon, 1987), but not at an expert level.

The transference of practical knowledge used by the novise rests, according to Polanyi (1946: 29-30), on rules and examples. The rules are relatively easy to describe and explain to a potential beginner. This type of knowledge can be codified and implemented in various types of files, databases, etc. Tacit knowledge is based initially on such rules, but through the development of this type of knowledge the focus shifts away from basic rules and towards being able to use certain quality criteria in action (Rolf, 1995: 113). When an individual has reached a competent level, he/she is able to use rules of thumb to perform the work (Wagner et al., 1999: 155-183). As the individual becomes more skilled in his/her profession or with a task, the basic rules become diffuse and the individual starts to apply rules of thumb. However, one must distinguish between a rule and the conditions that must be present for the rule to work (Rolf, 1995: 99). A rule of thumb may be defined as "a useful principle with wide application, not intended to be strictly accurate" (Morris, 1978: 1134).

Rules of thumb can facilitate achievements, but they can also prevent needed change and thereby inhibit a system's long-term survival. The effectiveness of rules of thumb in relation to tacit knowledge is therefore based on them being withdrawn when necessary changes are pressing.

Holistic causal understanding and deuteron-learning

The novice uses a lot of time trying to understand the causal pattern of a particular behaviour, while the person with some years of experience has an overall causal understanding of the situation. The person with some years of experience is able to diagnose a situation through an immediate situational awareness.

The structure of tacit knowledge concerns relations between parts, details and rules - the particular *from* which our attention is directed, to the totality *to* which our attention is directed. This is also the way in which the system is composed; a relationship between the parts that constitute the whole. The parts are subsidiary in relation to our attention, but it is these that constitute our starting point. That which is primary, or that which is the focus of our attention, is the whole. Thus, the structure of the system is analogous to the structure of tacit knowledge. Attention is directed from the parts to the whole (Scott, 1996: 52). Holistic causal understanding is, it might be said, a part-whole perspective, or context understanding (Augier, et.al., 2001), not unlike the way deutero- learning operates.

Deutero-learning is related to immediate context understanding (Bateson, 1972:294). This type of learning is linked to the competence of discriminating between different contexts in a given situation. Bateson writes about this type of learning: "a corrective change in the set of alternatives from which choice is made, or it is a change in how sequences of experience is punctuated" (Bateson,1972: 294). This may be looked upon as an intelligent response upon the different contexts which can happen in a given situation. Context understanding may also be thought of as a punctuation process. Bateson writes about this process: "We suggest that what is learned --- is a way of punctuating events. But a way of punctuating is not true or false. It is like a picture seen in an inkblot, it is neigther true or false. It is only a way of seeing the inkblot" (Bateson, 1972: 300).

Deutero-learning may also be looked upon as a way to redefine a problem. Contrasted to problem-solutions, deutero-learning focus problem-definition and a new framing of the problem. In this way deutero- learning may be understood as a foundation for innovation.

If one observes the parts (the particular) separately, then one will lose sight of the pattern. In other words, if one changes one's focal attention to a specific part of the whole, and then considers this part as if it were the whole, then the fragments are considered as representing the whole.

It is possible to make distinctions in the phenomenon we have under our focal attention, and thus create information. However, it is difficult to make distinctions of the phenomenon we have under our subsidiary attention, because it is difficult to create information directly from data. The focal awareness may be seen as a field of data where we know the code and can therefore systematize and structure it. We can create knowledge in such fields, which we cannot with regard to the phenomenon that we have under our subsidiary attention because the code is not known.

Subsidiary awareness and focal awareness are mutually exclusive activities. For instance, if a violin player shifts attention from the piece he/she is playing and interpreting to observing how he/she is holding the violin and playing the notes with his fingers, then he/she will most probably lose focus and be unable to play the piece in question skilfully (Polanyi, 1958: 56). Focal attention is conscious, while subsidiary attention may take on varying degrees of consciousness (Polanyi, 1958: 92). For instance, we may be conscious of our knee if we feel discomfort or pain when running. In the same way as primary and secondary attention is something we live in and live with, this also applies to our assumptions and beliefs, says Polanyi: "When we accept a certain set of pre-suppositions and use them as our interpretative framework, we may be said to dwell in them as we do in our own body" (Polanyi, 1958: 60).

The novice has his/her focal attention, for example, on a hammer, while the expert has his/her focal attention on the nail. The example is intended to illustrate that focal attention shifts as a function of experience over a period of time.

It seems that basic rules, by integrating with each other, create complex system behaviour, or according to Polanyi: "---the aim of a skilful performance is achieved by the observance of a set of rules which are not known as such to the person following them" (Polanyi, 1958: 49), and " ---the relationship of the particulars jointly forming a whole may be ineffable, even though all the particulars are explicitly specifiable" (Polanyi, 1958: 88).

Intuition and double-loop learning

A cognitive strategy on two levels seems to operate when developing tacit knowledge based on "learning by doing" (Arrow, 1962). On the lower level, automatic perceptual motor skills are developed, linking perception of the current state directly to an appropriate action strategy. On the upper level, errors are continuously revealed in relation to specific performance aims in an area of control. Therefore, the upper and lower limits are specified or developed through practice. Future conditions are anticipated and checked through practice against previous actions. New strategies are developed continuously in relation to new limits placed on situations in practice. A general procedure is thus gradually developed where the player ceases to connect to the lower level where the automatic perceptual skills were developed. This is what constitutes intuition as a type of tacit knowledge; it is woven into an individual's pattern of behaviour, which can't, or can but with great difficulty, be verbalized (Klein, 2003:26-28).

Let's consider a thought experiment. If a leader asks one of his/her experts, who have developed an innovative idea mainly based on tacit knowledge, to document the idea so that he/she has something concrete to submit to the management and directors, this would most likely reduce an idea of perhaps a high degree of complexity to something much simpler. In other words, the knowledge that the idea is based on will be levelled out – literally, because the whole is reduced to a small part, which is then presented and documented using explicit knowledge. This then results in the expert's innovative ideas being reduced to the skill level of the novice, because the novice mainly deals with explicit knowledge (Klein, 2003: 26-28; 304-305).

Double-loop learning is thought of as learning different contexts, i.e. to be able to make a distinction between them. Bateson, writes about double-loop learning: "the cases in which an entity gives at time 2 a different response from what it gave at time 1" (Bateson,1972:283). The same stimulus will in double-loop learning give different answers, because the person comprehend the context.

Understanding patterns and paradigmatic learning

The expert has a better sense of the information that is contained in a pattern than a novice or beginner. The expert is more skilled at decoding patterns, and patterns which connect with other patterns. He/she is thus able to deal with complex situations more skilfully than a novice (Dreyfus & Dreyfus, 1986). Understanding of patterns is closely related to intuition (Welsh & Lyons, 2001). A pattern is relatively stable over a period of time and may therefore be considered strategic. One type of pattern understanding that most people can relate to is to sense the mood of others by just by a glance at their facial expression. Facial expression, body language and non-verbal communication may be used to interpret a pattern and relate to a situation accordingly.

Pattern understanding results from the collection of a large number of facts and then interpreting these over a period of time into a more or less stable structure. In other words, the expert uses patterns in a target-oriented way. However, pattern development is something else; the development of patterns is more comparable to an induction process, while understanding patterns may be seen as a strategic process that occurs emergently[7] in the individual (Akbar & Mandurah, 2014:759-752).

---

[7] Emergent means here: "Let S be a system with composition A, i.e. the various components in addition to the way they are composed. If P is a property of S, P is emergent with regard to A, if and only if no components in A possess P; otherwise P is to be regarded as a resulting property with regards to A" (Bunge, 1977:97).

Patter understanding may be linked to paradigmatic learning in the following way.

In paradigmatic learning there is a total reorganizing of a persons way of thinking

Bateson writes about this type of learning: " a profound reorganization of character" (Bateson,1972: 303), not unlike changing of behaviour in response to pattern understanding.

How do different types of tacit knowledge and organizational learning influence innovation?

We know little about how tacit knowledge affects and influences innovation processes (Sheng, et.al., 2015). An interesting question is thus to what extent different types of tacit knowledge and different types of organizational learning promotes or inhibits a business's innovation ability .

Tacit knowledge can in some cases be a key barrier to innovation, such as when an organisation introduces a new production method or when a new product is being developed. This is because tacit knowledge usually is part of a long term learning process in a specific context, embodied in the structure of thinking, the way of thinking, and consequently functioning as a conservative element with regard to innovation.

Tacit knowledge, says Fleck (1996: 119): "is---the most crucial in restricting the social distribution of knowledge, and has been widely identified as a major constraint on the diffusion of both science and technology". This is also emphasised by Basalla (1988). On the other hand, tacit knowledge is a sort of organisational 'immune' system that prevents imitation by other social systems and promotes continuous improvement (Johannessen & Olsen, 2011). The function of tacit knowledge is then both conservative, i.e. stabilising the system, and also acts as a guard against imitation.

However, there are two types of tacit knowledge: rules of thumb and holistic causal understanding, both of which can slow down innovation (Johannessen & Olsen, 2011). This is because these types are closely linked to the rules, procedures and analysis; they are thus bound by the grip of history and experience, and operate as mechanisms that slow down the field of change.

Proposition 1: Rules of tumbs and single-loop learning inhibits innovation, but promotes continuous improvement.

Proposition 2: Holistic causal understanding and deutero-learning inhibits innovation, but promotes continuous improvement.

Intuition and pattern understanding encourage the innovation process. This is because these two types are connected to creativity and contextual understanding, dimensions that are prerequisites for innovation.

Proposition 3: Intuition and double loop learning promotes innovation.

Proposition 4: Pattern understanding and paradigmatic learning promotes innovation.

Analysis and implications

Tacit knowledge is bounded by a negative feedback factor, thus tacit knowledge promotes innovation only to a certain level and then declines. Solow (1997: 25) denotes this phenomenon as "bounded learning by doing". We, however, go a step further and assume that certain types of tacit knowledge have this effect on innovation.

Learning by doing, using and experimenting is here seen as generalised tacit knowledge. The more this generalised tacit knowledge is conservative, the more it is bounded by the negative feedback factor, and vice versa. The negative feedback factor function here in a way that stabilize the system and hinders innovation to change it. Imitation is part of continuous improvement and innovation, but only to a certain degree because tacit knowledge is difficult to imitate. Tacit knowledge then functions as a guard against imitation.

The generalised tacit knowledge in organisations can raise productivity to a higher level compared to competitors, because it can't be purchased in the market; it has to be developed inside an organisation, as a general rule. Thus tacit knowledge may be said to have three faces: one conservative that limits the continuous improvement process, a second that guards an organisation against imitation, and a third that promotes innovation.

The greater the intensity in the process of learning by doing, using and experimenting, the greater the productivity gained from the processes in an organisation. Thus, tacit knowledge plays a central role in the productivity of firms, both in steady state situations and even more so in a hypercompetitive market.

Since continuous improvements, innovations and the implementation of new technologies occur at different rates, they are connected non-linearly. The turbulent situation exists not only in the hypercompetitive market, but also inside organisations. To dampen internal turbulence, the conservative element of tacit knowledge is in operation.

The rate of productivity is limited by the rate of technological progress, continuous improvements and innovations. Continuous improvement, however, is linked to the stock of human capital (knowledge).

In this chapter we have argued that certain types of tacit knowledge and organizational learning, inhibit innovation because they are related to a conservative element of tacit knowledge. However, these types of tacit knowledge and organizational learning can promote continuous improvements.

In the chapter, the types of tacit knowledge that we have termed intuition and understanding of patterns may be said to promote innovation because they are connected to double loop learning and paradigmatic learning creativity, which are linked to contextual understanding and deep specialization; dimensions that are prerequisites for innovation.

Understood in this way, the typology of tacit knowledge and organizational learning (fig. 1) is an active tool for managing organizations towards, respectively, continuous improvement and innovation.

Conclusion

The typology (Fig. 1) and the propositions may be the answer to our research question. Used by management it can help to clarify the information vacuum that exists in strategic processes between decision makers and those who possess various kinds of tacit knowledge. If one, in the context of strategy, does not pay attention to tacit knowledge but bases activities on documented explicit knowledge, one risks using the knowledge of novices as a premise and not the knowledge of experts. It thus reduces the organisation's forum of knowledge, which becomes concerned mainly with the novice's level of knowledge. In this context one may say that explicit knowledge is an island surrounded by and based on tacit knowledge processes and tacit knowledge. The statement that one is no stronger than one's weakest link is realized with full effect in such a strategy. The organisation employs in this way a small part of the knowledge that is available within the organisation in its strategic processes, and becomes worse off than it really needs to be. One could say that organizations in this way are dumber than they have to be.

References

Akbar, H. & Mandurah, S. (2014). Project-conceptualisation in technological innovations: A knowledge-based perspective, International Journal of Project Management, 32, 5:759-772.

Amirkhani, A.h. &Heydari, H. (2015). The study on the role of sharing tacit knowledge in psychological empowerment of medical staff
of the social security organization, Journal of Management Sciences, 1,

8:167-174.

Anzai,Y. & Simon, H.A. (1979). The theory of learning by doing,

Psychological, Review,86:124-140.

Argyris, C. (1999). Tacit knowledge and management, In Sternberg, R. & Horvath, J.A. (eds.). Tacit knowledge in professional practice, Lawrence Erlbaum, London. S.123-141.

Argyris, C. & Schøn, D.(1978). Organizational Learning, A Theory of

actionPerspective, Addison Wesley, Reading, Mass.

Arrow, K.J. (1962). The economic implications of learning by doing,

Review of Economic Studies, 29:155-173.

Augier, M.: Syed, Z.; Shariq, M. & Vendelø, T. (2001). Understanding context: its emergence, transformation and role in tacit knowledge sharing, Journal of Knowledge Management, 5, 2:125-137

Basalla, G. (1988). The evolution of technology, Cambridge University Press, Cambridge.

Bateson,G. (1972). Steps to an ecology of mind, Intex Books, London.

Bunge, M. (1977). Treatise on basic philosophy. Vol. 3. Ontology I: The furniture of the world. Dordrecht, Holland: D. Reidel.

Bunge, M. (1985). Philosophy of Science and Technology, Part I, Reidel, Dordrecht.

Bunge, M. (1998). Philosophy of science: From problem to theory, Volume one, Transaction Publishers, New Jersey.

Bush, P.B. (2008). Tacit knowledge and organizational learning, Macquarie University Australia, Hershey.

Cannon, D. (2002). Constructing Polanyis tacit knowing as knowing by acquaintance rather than knowing by representation, Tradition and Discovery, 29, 2:26-43.

Collins, H. (2010). Tacit and explicit knowledge, The University of Chicago Press, Chicago.

Contini, F. & Lanzara, G.F. (eds.) (2008). ICT and innovation in the public sector, Palgrave, London.

Donate, M.J. & de Pablo, J.D.S. (2015). The role of knowledge-oriented leadership in knowledge management practices and innovation, Journal of Business Research, 68, 2: 360-370.

Dreyfus, H.L. & Dreyfus, S.E. (1986). Mind over machine: The power of human intuition and expertice in the era of the computer, Free Press, New York.

Fleck, J. (1996). Informal information flow and the nature of expertice in financial services, International Journal of Technology Management, 11, 1-2: 104-128.

Gangi, di, P.M. & Wasko, M. (2009). Open innovation through online communities, In King, W.R. Knowledge management and organizational learning, Springer, London. S.199-213.

Garavan, T,N. & McGuire, D. (2015). Reclaiming the "D" in HRD: A typology of development conceptualizations, Antecedents, and outcomes, Human Resource Development Review, online publishing, 28. Sept.

Grillitsch, M. & Rekers, J.V. (2015). How does multi-scalar institutional change affect localized learning processes? A case study of the med-tech sector in southern Sweeden, Environment and Planning, Online Publishing, 18. Sept.

Johannessen, J-A.; Olsen, B. & Lumkin, G.T. (2001). Innovation as newness: what is new, how new, and new to whom?, European Journal of Innovation Management, 4, 1:20 -31.

Johannessen, J-A. & Olsen, B. (2011) Aspects of a cybernetic theory of tacit knowledge and innovation", Kybernetes, 40,1 and 2:141 – 165.

Kahnemann, D. & Klein, G. (2009). Conditions for intuitive expertise: A failure to disagree, American Psycologist, 64, 6:515-526.

King, W.R. (2009). Basic concepts of knowledge management, In King, W.R. Knowledge management and organizational learning, Springer, London. S. 1.13.

Klein, G. (1998). Sources of power: How people make decisionsMIT Press, Cambridge, MA.

Klein, G. (2003). The power of intuition, Currency Doubleday, New York.

Lam, A. (2000). Tacit knowledge, organizational learning and societal institutions: An integrated framework, Organization Studies, 21, 3:487-513.

Little, D. (1995). Learning by dialogue: The dependence of learner autonomy on teacher autonomy, System, 23, 2: 171-181.

Marchant, E. & Robinson, J. (1999). Is knowing the tax code all it takes to be a tax expert? In Sternberg, R. & Horvath, J.A. (eds.). Tacit knowledge in professional practice, Lawrence Erlbaum, London. S.3-21.

Mascitelli, R. (2000). From experience: Harnessing tacit knowledge to achieve breakthrough innovation, The Journal of Product Innovation Management, 17, 3:179-193.

Matte, F. & Cooren, F. (2015). Learning as dialogue, I Filliettaz, L. & Billett, S. (eds.). Francophone Perspectives of learning through work, Springer, Berlin. S. 169-181.

Molander, B. (1993). Kunskap i handling, Daidalos, Gøteborg.

Morris, W. (ed.). (1978). The american herritage dictionary of the english language, Houghton Mifflin, Boston.

Nishinaka, M.; Umemoto, K. & Kohda, Y. (2015). Emergence of common tacit knowledge in an international IT project: A case study between Japan and Singapore, International Journal of Managing Projects in Business, Vol. 8, 3:533 – 551.

Nonaka, I. (1991). The knowledge creating company, Harvard Business Review, 69, 6: 96- 104.

Nonaka, I. (1994). A dynamic theory of organizational knowledge creation, Organizational Science, 5, 1: 14-37.

Nonaka, I. & Takeuchi, H. (1995). The Knowledge Creating Company, Oxford University Press, Oxford.

Nonaka, I. & Ichijo, K. (1997). Creating knowledge in the process organization: A comment on Denisons chapter, In Walsh, J.P. & Huff, A.S. (eds.). Advancement in Strategic Management, Vol. 14: 45-52, JAI-Press, New York.

Polanyi, M. (1946). Science, faith and society, Oxford University Press, Oxford.

Polanyi, M. (1958). Personal knowledge, Routledge & Kegan Paul, London.

Polanyi, M. (2009). The tacit dimention, The University of

Chicago Press, Chicago.

Robinson, J.A. (1996). Why do piano motor skills work better if they are tacit and automatic, Chapter presented at making tacit knowledge explicit, Japan: Keio University.

Rolf, B. (1995). Profession, tradition och tyst kunskap, Nya Doxa, Nora, Sverige

Rosenberg, N. (1982). Inside the black box: Technology and economics, Cambridge University Press, Cambridge.

Scott, R.W. (1995). Institutions and organizations, Sage, London.

Schøn, D. (1987). Educating the reflective practioner, Jossey-Bass, London.

Schøn, D. (1988). Designing: Rules, types and worlds, Design Studies, Vol. 9: 181-190.

Sheng, M.L. Nathaniel; Hartmann, N.; Chen, Q., & Chen, I. (*2015*). The Synergetic Effect of Multinational Corporation Management's Social Cognitive Capability on Tacit-Knowledge Management: Product Innovation Ability Insights from Asia. Journal of International Marketing, 2015, 23, 2:94-110.

Simon, H.A. (1987). Making management decisions: The role of intuition and emotion, Academy of Management Executive, 1: 57-64.

Solow, R.M. (1997). Learning from learning by doing: Lessons for economic growth. Stanford University Press. Stanford: California.

Sveiby, K.E. (1997). The new organizational wealth: Managing & measuring knowledge-based assets, Berrett-Koehler Publisher, San Francisco.

Wagner, R.K. (1987). Tacit knowledge in everyday intelligent behavior, Journal of

Personality and Social Psychology, 52: 1236-1247.

Wagner, R.K., Sujan, H., Sujan, M., Rashotte, C.A. & Sternberg, R.J. (1999). Tacit

knowledge in sales, in Sternberg, R. & Horvath, J.A. (eds.). (s. 155-183). Tacit knowledge in professional practice, Lawrence Erlbaum Associates, London.

Welsh, I. & Lyons,M. (2001). Evidence-based care and the case for intuition and tacit knowledge in clinical assessment and decision making in mental health nursing practice: an empirical contribution to the debate, Journal of Psychiatric andMental Health Nursing, 8, 4:299-305

Chapter 4 Innovation and entrepreneurial policy

Introduction

Entrepreneurship and innovation policy has been studied at national level (Lundstrom & Stevenson, 2010), but to a lesser extent at organizational level (Carayannis, et al., 2015: 262-264). Further, it poses a problem that we do not have a theory than can guide research and practices at organizational level in the development of entrepreneurship and innovation policy.

Policy may be understood as principles, guidelines or models that are intended to guide decisions, or to build or develop something for different objectives (Desrochers & Sautet, 2008). Simon (1962) expresses very clearly the view that modelling can be used to develop policy at different levels. According to Simon, we construct and develop models, because we wish to understand the consequences of one decision against another (Simon 1988).

In the light of what is described here, a policy may be understood as a model that is developed and applied for the purposes of making decisions in order to achieve particular goals, or to moderate the effects of something that we cannot fully control (Simon, 1977; 1991).

One of the points of future research and policy modelling is "...

describing, explaining, predicting, exploring and interpreting future developments and its consequences, as the result of actions and decisions in the present." (Berkhout, et al., 2007:74). Against this background, policy models may be defined as decision models that are intended to describe, explain, predict, research and/or interpret future trends and their consequences.

This chapter is concerned with policy at organizational level. The question we are investigating is: How can we develop policy models for entrepreneurship and innovation at organizational level?

This chapter will be consistent in its use of the term "entrepreneurship", where other authors may have used terms such as, intrapreneurship, strategic entrepreneurship, intrapreneurial intensity, corporate entrepreneurship, etc. This is done, because we aim to simplify the use of terminology, making the chapter more accessible to those involved with practical implementation, so that they are able to understand the main ideas in the chapter. In our application of the entrepreneurship concept, we are in agreement with Schumpeter's first use of the concept: "Schumpeter's entrepreneur can operate inside an enterprise or independently" (Andersen, 2009; 2011); also, Schumpeter writes, "The carrying out of new combinations, the individuals whose function is to carry them out we call entrepreneurs" (Schumpeter, 1934: 74-75), and they are: "all who actually fulfil the function by which we define the concept, even if they are, as is becoming the rule, dependent employees of a company" (op. cit.).

The focus of innovation and entrepreneurship is value creation (Hamel, 2002; 2012; Kirzner, 1973;1979;1982; 1985;1999), and value creation can exist at various levels.

We define value creation as all the activities and processes that address human needs (Baird & Henderson, 2001, Johannessen & Olsen, 2010).

Value creation generally involves a process of co-creation (Prahalad & Ramaswamy, 2004: 7-17). The classic view of value creation is that it occurs within an individual company. Accordingly, the situation varies depending on the situation in the individual company (Reinmoell & Reinmoeller, 2015). Each company devotes efforts to developing different process- and product-related innovations, with a focus on its own internal processes. The new policy models for innovation and entrepreneurship extend the boundaries, and view the business in the context of the larger system of which it is a part (Shane & Venkataraman, 2000; Lundstrøm & Stevenson, 2010). Value creation thus occurs in a systemic interaction between different social systems at different levels (Prahalad & Ramaswamy, 2004: 15). This complexity is one of the reasons why there is a greater need now to develop policy models for entrepreneurship and innovation. Another reason is that both innovation and entrepreneurship are directly associated with economic growth and employment (Stevenson & Jarillo, 1990; Hamel, 2012; Kirzner, 1982;1985).

Change and uncertainty are both concepts associated with entrepreneurship and innovation. In general, one can say that innovation creates "gaps" in the market by introducing change and uncertainty, while entrepreneurship fills the "gaps", bringing it back towards stability. In this fashion, innovation and entrepreneurship have two different functions in a market. Innovation creates "gaps" in the market and promotes turbulence. The entrepreneurs then fill the "gaps" and bring back stability and equilibrium to the market. This dual function of innovation and entrepreneurship can in its consequences be said to reduce market uncertainty.

Schumpeter's entrepreneur is one who participates in an economic process in order to develop new combinations (Kirzner, 1973; 1982; 1985; 1999). In Schumpeter's view, entrepreneurial action leads to creative destruction (Schumpeter, 1934). It is namely creative destruction that leads to disequilibrium in the market. Indeed, the more innovations that are introduced, the greater the likelihood of disequilibrium in the market. One can also imagine that the more innovations introduced in the market, the greater the likelihood of temporary economic crises, because the market can not adapt quickly enough.

Following Schumpeter's idea of creative destruction, Casson

(1982, 1991, 1993) introduced the importance of culture in understanding entrepreneurial action. However, Simon (1991) focuses on the importance of emotion and intuition. Kirzner (1973; 1979; 1985; 1999) returned to the ideas of the Austrian school when considering the importance of the individual behind entrepreneurial processes, especially the individual entrepreneur who seeks knowledge to develop innovations. In all of these perspectives, it is the entrepreneur who brings back equilibrium to the market after innovations have caused disequilibrium. To express this more broadly, it may be said that innovation tends to create temporary economic crises, while entrepreneurship deals with the crises and enables us to emerge from them. Consequently, it is important to have policy models for both innovation and entrepreneurship.

Research on entrepreneurship has gone from the personal and psychological characteristics of the entrepreneur (Alsos & Kolvereid, 1998:101-114) to a more behavioural approach, focusing on how the entrepreneur discovers and exploits opportunities, how they act, and the consequences of their actions (Stevenson & Jarillo, 1990). In this regard, the view of knowledge of Schumpeter and Kirzner is interesting. While Schumpeter focuses on explicit knowledge, Kirzner's view (1973; 1999), with his concept of "entrepreneurial alertness", may be more closely linked to tacit knowledge. Kirzner extends the reach beyond tacit knowledge, and refers to a knowledge domain where we "do not even know that we do not know", which is termed here "hidden knowledge" (Kirzner, 1973; 1982; 1999).

Kirzner's perspective may explain why some are able to see and exploit opportunities while others are unable to. This perspective may also provide an explanation why some research (Carter et al., 1996) shows that extensive planning often inhibits entrepreneurial success, rather than promoting it. On the basis of this research, it is reasonable to assume that action based on tacit knowledge, and Kirzner's concept "hidden knowledge", explain why some succeed while others fail.

A further explanation regarding the importance of using the two types of knowledge (tacit and hidden) to ensure success may be found in research that indicates that experience plays a role in success (Cooper, et al., 1989, 1994). Tacit knowledge and hidden knowledge are distinct but related. They are related in the sense that they both are associated with experience. They are distinct because they belong to two different domains of knowledge. With our focus on tacit knowledge and hidden knowledge, the individual entrepreneur's past experience may thus determine future success. Furthermore, the entrepreneur's social contacts and interaction in these networks is a contributing factor to success, because his "entrepreneurial alertness" (Kirzner, 1979; 1985) is strengthened.

The above description may be summarized in the following policy model of entrepreneurship and innovation.

Fig. 1. Analytical policy model of entrepreneurship and innovation at organizational level.

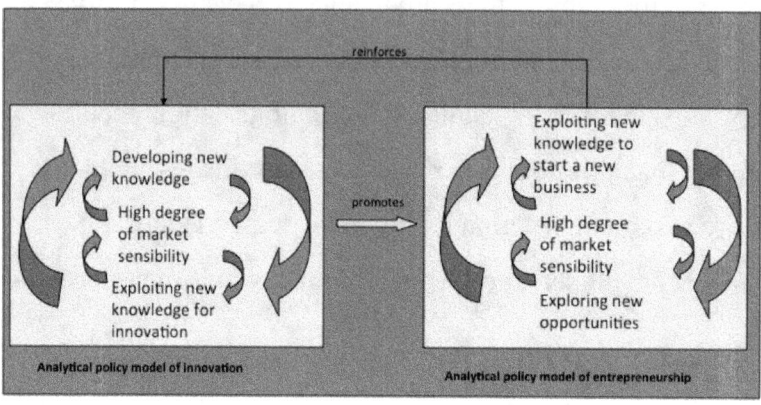

Explanation of the analytical policy model

If we break down this analytical policy model into two distinct but related policy models, the result is three loops that form the conceptual policy model of entrepreneurship and three loops that form the conceptual policy model of innovation. The conceptual policy model of entrepreneurship is formed of the three concepts on the right-hand side of the analytical model: exploiting new knowledge, market sensibility and exploring new opportunities. The three entrepreneurial loops are thus:

1. "Entrepreneurial drive" (exploiting new knowledge to start a business and a high degree of market sensibility)
2. "Innovative entrepreneurial drive" (exploiting new knowledge to start a business and exploring new opportunities)
3. "Co-operation drive" (exploring new opportunities and a high degree of market sensibility).

The policy model of innovation is formed by the three concepts on the left-hand side of the analytical policy model: developing new knowledge, a high degree of market sensibility and exploiting new knowledge. The three innovation loops are thus:

1. "Market drive" (developing new knowledge and a high degree of market sensibility)
2. "Technology push" (developing new knowledge and applying new knowledge to achieve innovation)
3. "Customer drive" (applying new knowledge to achieve innovation and market sensibility)

An essential point of the six loops in this analytical policy model is precisely that they are loops and thus do not constitute a linear model; i.e. a circle has no beginning or end. Development may start at any point in any of the six loops. For example, it is not necessarily the case that one starts in the three innovation loops developing new knowledge and then apply this knowledge to develop and innovate a product that is launched on the market.

Such policy thinking is represented in the classic linear model, not the loop-style or interaction model as shown in Fig. 1. The linear models may be understood by referring to Newton's physics (Capra, 2010: 40-56). The circular or interactive models may be traced back to Gregory Bateson's feedback loops (Bateson, 1972) and Karl Weick's interactive and circular thinking (Weick, 1979).

In Fig. 1 it's not the case that knowledge development or its utilization are at one end of the process and the market and opportunities are at the other. The point is that the analytical policy model (as shown in Fig. 1) is circular; and in a circle, it is immaterial where one begins, because following a circular path will eventually complete the circular process.

We choose in the following to focus on market sensibility and the exploration of new opportunities (shown in Fig. 1), because the development, application and exploitation of new knowledge is a relatively well-known and well-examined topic in relation to both entrepreneurship and innovation (Baird & Henderson, 2001; Brynjolfsson & McAfee, 2014; Innerarity, 2012; Hamel, 2012).

Market sensibility

A fundamental idea behind all innovation is that new ideas emerge through the combination of existing knowledge that is then accepted by the market (Hamel, 2012; Christensen, 1997; Johannessen, et al., 2001:20-31). However, the market is not the only selection mechanism in the innovation process (Gershuny, J. & Fisher, K., 2014).

Another selection method is the screening of ideas before an attempt is made to put them on the market (Prahalad & Krishnan, 2008). These screening methods are just as important to focus on as the market, because ideas that may have a huge market potential can sometimes be filtered out before they are given the opportunity to be tested in the market (Prahalad & Ramaswamy, 2004). This may also be derived from Hamel's Law of Innovation, which states that for every 1,000 new ideas, only one or two will turn out to be an innovation (Hamel, 2002; 2012). On the other hand, ideas that may not have such a large market potential slip through the screening and are put into production (Pyöriä, 2005). The latter leads to a reduction in revenues, while the former leads to lost opportunities (Ramaswamy & Ozcan, 2014). A simple social mechanism to prevent this from happening is that the people who evaluate ideas should justify the reasons for rejections, as well as any ideas they allow to pass through. When reasons for rejecting and accepting ideas do not have to be given, there will always be the danger that motives other than innovation and value creation may get on the agenda (Reinhardt, et al., 2011).

The policy implications of this reflection are the following:

1. The reasons given for accepting/rejecting ideas must be related to value creation in an organization.

2. There must be common rules for making decisions that involve rejecting ideas.
3. There must be explicit procedures for interaction between the originator of ideas and the decision makers.
4. A refusal must always be justified in relation to the market, because the reason given can then possibly be tested in relation to the market.

Innovation and entrepreneurship are directly linked to value creation for individual organizations and society. Therefore, the rules and procedures for the grounds of the rejection of ideas are essential. Metaphorically, this may be expressed by saying "It's just as easy to tear down an unfinished picture as it is to reject an unfinished idea." Therefore, the reasons for rejection must follow clear rules and procedures, which will increase the likelihood that an idea can be developed so that its value creation potential is reached.

The importance of market sensibility with regard to innovation and entrepreneurship is emphasized by Kirzner (1973; 1979; 1985); however, he says nothing about how market sensibility can be developed in individual enterprises.

If we take the position that the rate of change and turbulence will increase in the global knowledge economy, where high-tech production is central (Baird & Henderson, 2001; Azmat, et al., 2012), then planning and classical strategic thinking will be of less importance, because the results of such processes take a long time and the terrain changes more rapidly than before (Helfat, et al, 2007).

If the rate of change increases dramatically, it seems reasonable to assume that we can rely on our fundamental experience to a lesser extent. If we further assume, to follow this line of thinking to its conclusion, that the value of our experience collapse, then it seems reasonable to assume that new ways of relating to the future will emerge (White & Younger, 2013). Ideas, expectations and greater understanding of patterns will become more significant, although the Iron Law of History will still affect our perception of the future (Jansen, et al., 2006). The Iron Law of History is understood here as: our experience governs our perception, expectations and understanding of patterns, although it may have no real relevance for the present. In other words, rules and procedures that once were of great relevance, but which have become irrelevant due to the passage of time, still operate in practice.

One of the immediate results that occurs when the relevance of our fundamental experience collapses is many businesses will grasp at strategies that once produced good results, i.e. they are governed by the Iron Law of History. The point here, though, is that when businesses stick to old methods at a time when the rate of change and complexity increases, their work will become more detailed but will reflect new realities less and less. Maier (2015) has also reached similar conclusions, but he focuses on the Iron

Law of History from a different perspective, namely how to explore opportunities, while maintaining and utilizing current processes.

Market sensibility may be categorized into demand and needs. Demand categories may be divided into two types: concept testing and pilot testing. Concept testing refers to various methods of market research which aim to uncover the interests and preferences of customers and potential customers. This is done at an early stage of an idea's life cycle (de Bont, 1992). Various methods exist for this technique (Klink & Athaide, 2006). When the concept eventually reaches a more mature stage, a pilot may be developed based on the refined concept. It is here that the new concept is tested in relation to existing products and services in the market.

Needs assessments may also be divided into two types: structural analogies and pattern detection. Pattern detection considers latent needs and needs embodied in underlying trends (Urban et al., 1997). Structural analogies examine needs by comparing existing products and services in relation to new products and services.

Demand-oriented and needs-oriented approaches are not mutually exclusive, but complement each other to increase a business's market sensibility, and they also relate to exploring new opportunities.

Exploring new opportunities

Ideas, expectations, intuition and understanding of patterns may be related to the domain of hidden knowledge that deals with "what we do not know we do not know", which Kirzner (1982: 272), amongst others, describes as an important domain for entrepreneurship and innovation.

Kirzner (Ibid) says that it is in this area of knowledge "--- entrepreneurial profit opportunities exist." Thomsen (1992: 61) describes hidden knowledge as: "--- previously unthought-of knowledge."

However, this scope of opportunities may be subject to social mechanisms that restrict the scope of opportunities. One of the most prominent limiting factors is related to power and position in organizations (Rios, 2012). In any organization, there will be many individuals whose influence is linked to processes related to the Iron Law of History (Robertson, 2015). These individuals will probably stand to lose their positions and power in a situation where the scope of opportunities is large, when the values and relevance of experience collapses, and new policy models for innovation and entrepreneurship are developed. It is therefore understandable that they will oppose a shift away from processes governed by the Iron Law of History and towards processes characterized by an open scope of opportunities. Kahneman and Tversky's prospect theory also provides an explanation why they resist change (Kahneman, 2011; Kahneman & Tversky, 1999; 2000; 2008a; 2000b).

A possible solution at policy level, to avoid the Iron Law of History from operating in organizations, is to use open networks for innovation and entrepreneurship. In an open network, position and power will not be able to make its influence felt to the same extent. Open networks extend beyond the business boundaries, and work in the same way as open innovation models (Chesbrough, 2003; Kirschbaum, 2005). Open networks also enable a larger degree of creativity, which Von Hippel (2005) has shown with his concept "democratizing innovation". This is one of the reasons why one should look to other people than the so-called "lead users" when innovation projects are implemented. The probability that a new perspective makes a breakthrough is greater in open than in closed internal networks. The prerequisite for this to work is that top management has given decision-making powers to the open network (Von Hippel, 1986; 2005; Brynjolfsson & McAfee, 2014).

Focusing on lead users is not the best approach when dealing with hidden knowledge. In this respect, we are on a collision course with von Hippel's view of "lead users" (Von Hippel, 1986). However, a "lead users" approach may be used at a later stage in the development of a product, not when uncovering hidden knowledge.

If one focuses exclusively on the future to ensure the success of innovation projects, as van der Duin (2006) claims is necessary, then all that will emerge will be the past in various guises, because the Iron Law of History operates on the present and prevents creative insight concerning future projects. Moreover, the relevance of our fundamental experience collapses and the future will tend to be just an extrapolation of known quantities.

Attention must rather be directed toward creating what you want to appear in the future (Ackoff, 1982). One can create the future through at least two processes: firstly, active application of the scope of opportunities. Here the point is that businesses create their own future and do not adapt to what others have created (Ackoff, 1982). To achieve this, it is important to use open networks, which are crucial social mechanisms in this context (Chesbrough, 2003). Furthermore, the future is created through ideas, expectations, intuition and understanding of patterns (Cooper, 1980). Intuition is nothing other than tacit knowledge at a strategically high level (Johannessen & Olsen, 2011), a type of knowledge that may be developed and managed by organizations to promote innovation and entrepreneurship.

The scope of opportunity and the future is also created when an organization is able to "--- visualize or identify pictures of future opportunities, and turn them into reality" (Johannessen et al., 1999: 18). The visualization is achieved by continually exploring new opportunities and developing an extreme form of market sensibility.

The link between market sensibility and the scope of opportunities

Market sensibility will always be related to various time horizons, which may differ from industry to industry. For instance, what may seem like a long period of time in the electronics industry may be considered short in the pharmaceutical industry. The different types of innovation and entrepreneurship projects, and the different time horizons of various industries, suggest that the people who develop policy models in the individual enterprises must be closely linked to those concerned with the development of knowledge in the scope of opportunities. This reinforces the idea of open networks.

The future of an individual organization is created in this way as an interaction between policy models and the scope of opportunity as it is developed along the relevant time horizon. Open networks may be understood as a type of knowledge sharing. Hidden knowledge is constituted in such a way that it is hidden for some but accessible to others. When one reflects on hidden knowledge in open networks, more of the hidden knowledge domain steadily becomes visible. If this reflection had not been carried out, then the hidden knowledge would remain hidden and an entrepreneurial opportunity would have been lost. Open networks are therefore a social mechanism that can uncover hidden knowledge and stimulate entrepreneurship.

If we look at entrepreneurship as the process in which: "opportunities to create future goods and services are discovered, evaluated and exploited" (Shane & Venkataraman, 2000:218), then hidden knowledge is the key to the entrepreneurial process.

Developments towards a theory of entrepreneurship and innovation policy at organizational level

By "theory" we mean a system of propositions (Bunge, 1977; 1985; 1998).

There are three main categories of interaction in Fig. 1:

Integration I: Innovation integration

Innovation integration will ensure a strong link between the three innovation loops.

Integration II: Entrepreneurship integration

Entrepreneurship integration will ensure that there is a strong link between the three entrepreneurship loops.

Integration III: Innovation and entrepreneurship integration

Integration III will ensure a strong link between innovation integration on the one hand and entrepreneurship integration on the other hand.

Proposition 1: The stronger the degree of integration between the three innovation loops in Integration I, the greater the likelihood that the rate of innovation will increase.

Proposition 2: The stronger the degree of integration between the three entrepreneurship loops in Integration II, the greater the likelihood that the rate of entrepreneurship will increase.

Proposition 3: The stronger the degree of integration between the innovation loops and the entrepreneurship loops in Integration III, the greater the likelihood that innovative entrepreneurship[8] will increase.

Analysis and implications of the three propositions

The analytical policy model in Fig. 1 has clear organizational consequences. One such consequence is pointed out by Kanter (2006), who underlines the need of resolving hierarchical management and control mechanisms to promote the development of "bottom up" commitment and enthusiasm, which may lead to

---

[8] Innovative entrepreneurship concerns enterprises that start up on the basis of an innovative idea.

innovation and entrepreneurship.

A second consequence is a shift from functional organization to frontline organization. In front-line organization, responsibility, information, decision-making authority and competence, etc., are transferred from the upper level in the hierarchy to the front line, i.e. those who are in direct contact with the user, customer, patient, student, etc. (Johannessen & Olsen, 2010). In front-line organization, the boundaries of classical functional organization are dissolved, the hierarchical and bureaucratic structure is greatly de-emphasised, while the system is organized on the basis of the customer's encounter with those who are in the front line.

Obviously, certain individuals specialise in front line organization as well. The point is simply that their specialization does not determine the way a business organizes itself, as is the case to a great extent with functional organization. This may provide one explanation of the three propositions, namely, that it seems reasonable to assume that front-line organization may become the dominant principle in knowledge organizations.

A third but related consequence of functional organization is that people specialize precisely in relation to how businesses are organized. Businesses are not organized according to people's specialization in front-line organization, but based on customers' needs and demands, and organize the business in relation to this interaction. This has clear implications for innovation and entrepreneurship in businesses, which the three propositions attempt to say something about.

A fourth organizational consequence of Integration III is that front line organization develops what may be termed front line teams – teams that are organized without functional boundaries. Furthermore, customers / users are a part of these teams. One of the reasons for this way of organizing teams is that a good deal of research shows that the integration of customers / users in the innovation process promotes value creation for businesses (Von Hippel, 2005 Kanter, 2006 Chesbrough, 2003).

A fifth consequence of the policy model in Fig. 1 and the three propositions is that the linear innovation models are given less emphasis. The linear model may be explained figuratively by the use of pipelines which are normally used (literally speaking) for transporting liquids and gasses. Yet there is nothing to suggest that knowledge development and sharing can be made effective along such a linear "pipeline", i.e. starting with R&D at point A, and moving then to point B in a process of use and exploitation (see Figure 1). In writing about innovation, many attempts have been made to improve on the "pipeline" metaphor. For instance, Chesbrough (2003) attempts this by using open innovation models. However, this is still a linear model. The difference is just that you start at the other end, namely with the "stakeholders" in the outside world. Kirschbaum (2005) also attempts to improve upon the metaphor by using the terms "spin-in" and "spin-out", which also describes a linear model but one based on an interaction between first starting at one end of the "pipeline", then switching over to the other end. Although metaphors are important to facilitate our understanding, they are not real; yet they can be real in their consequences when used in practice.

One of the weaknesses of linear thinking and the "pipeline" metaphor is that they are unable to incorporate what we know about the importance of feedback and feedforward mechanisms (expectation mechanism). However, the analytical innovation and entrepreneurship model in Fig. 1, and the three propositions, incorporate feedback, feedforward, and pullback[9] mechanisms which are designed into it. The "spin in" and "spin out" thinking of Kirschbaum may also be used effectively in the analytical innovation and entrepreneurship model. One of the results of such thinking is that existing elements of knowledge can become new knowledge when they are combined with each other, while simultaneously eyeing practical contexts. This may be termed innovation's oblique intention, i.e. looking to the side to understand what's coming in the future. This interactive and circular understanding constitutes the dominant logic in Fig. 1 and the three propositions.

---

[9] Pullback may by explained in relation to a painter who focuses on a part of a painting to gain an understanding of how part and whole are related.

Conclusion

We started with the question (problem approach): How can we develop policy models of entrepreneurship and innovation at organizational level (in the global knowledge economy)?

The interaction between the three loops that form the conceptual policy model of entrepreneurship, and the three loops that form the conceptual policy model of innovation (Fig. 1) are essential for value creation, which is the focus of both innovation and entrepreneurship.

To promote a greater degree of integration between the three innovation loops and three entrepreneurship loops in Fig. 1, one can imagine innovation and entrepreneurship as operating on three levels; individual, team and organizational levels.

At the individual level the focus is on creative strategies, methods and techniques, so the individual will be able to continually explore new opportunities. At the team level, the focus is on complementary expertise when groups are formed; all four types of knowledge mentioned above will be taken into account. At the organizational level, it becomes important to organize the double loop. First, innovation is organized as a separate functional unit where there is a focus on the importance of development and application of new knowledge for innovation in order to promote market sensibility. Then the focus will be on the utilization of knowledge to establish a business and also to explore new opportunities to increase market sensibility. Finally, the two loops are organized to promote Integration III, which will increase value creation.

References

Ackoff, R.L. (1982). Creating the corporate future, John Wiley & Sons, New York.

Alsos, G.A. & Kolvereid, L. (1998). The Business Gestation Process of Novice, Serial, and Parallel Business Founders, Entrepreneurship, Theory and Practice, 22, 4: 101-114.

Andersen, E. (2009). Schumpeter's Evolutionary Economics: A Theoretical, Historical and Statistical Analysis of the Engine of Capitalism, Anthem Press, London.

Andersen, E.S (2011). Joseph A. Schumpeter: A Theory of Social and Economic Evolution (Great Thinkers in Economics), Palgrave, London.

Azmat, G.; Manning, A. & Van Reenen, J. (2012). Privatization and the Decline of the Labour's Share: International Evidence from Network Industries, Economica, 79:470-492.

Baird,L. & Henderson, J.C. (2001). The Knowledge Engine, Berrett-Koehler, San Francisco.

Bateson, G. (1972). Steps to an ecology of mind,

Basalla, G. (2001). The evolution of technology, Cambridge University Press, Cambridge.

Berkhout, G.; Van den Duin, P.; Hartman, D. & Ortt, R. (2007). The cyclic nature of innovation: Connecting hard sciences with soft values, Elsevier, Amsterdam.

Brynjolfsson, E. & McAfee, A. (2014). The Second Machine Age, W.W. Norton, New York.

Bunge, M. (1977). Treatise on basic philosophy. Vol. 3. Ontology I: The furniture of the world. Dordrecht, Holland: D. Reidel.

Bunge, M. (1985). Philosophy of Science and Technology, Part I, Reidel, Dordrecht.

Bunge, M. (1998). Philosophy of science: From problem to theory, Volume one, Transaction Publishers, New Jersey.

Capra, F. (2010). The turning point, Flamingo, New York.

Carayannis, E.G.; Samara, E.T. & Bokouros, Y.L. (2015). Innovation and entrepreneurship: Theory, policy and practice, Springer, Berlin.

Carter, N.M.; Gartner, W.B. & Reynolds, P.D. (1996). Exploring start-up event sequences, Journal of Business Venturing, 11:151-166.

Casson, M. (1982). The entrepreneur. An economic theory, Martin Robinson, Oxford.

Casson, M. (1991). The economic of business culture, Oxford University Press, Oxford.

Casson, M. (1993). Entrepreneurship and business culture, I Brown, J. & Rose, M.B. (eds.). Entrepreneurship, networks and modern business, Manchester University Press, Manchester.

Chesbrough, H. (2003). Open innovation. The new imperative for creating and profiting from technology, Harvard Business School Press, Boston.

Christensen, C.M. (1997). The Innovator's Dilemma: When New Technologies Cause Great Firms to Fail. Boston: Harvard Business School Press.

Cooper, A.C.; Noo, C.Y. & Duakelberg, W.C. (1989). Entrepreneurship and the initial size of firms, Journal of Business Venturing, 4: 317-332.

Cooper, A.C.; Gimeno-Gascon, F.J. & Woo, C.Y. (1994). Initial human and financial capital predictors of new venture performance, Journal of Business Venturing, 9: 371-395.

Cooper, R.G. (1980). Project newprod: factors in the new product success, European Journal of Marketing, 14, 5/6: 277-291.

De Bont, C.J.P.M. (1992). Consumer evolutions of early

product-concepts, Delf University Press, Delft.

Desrochers, P. & Sautet, F. (2008). Entrepreneurial Policy: The Case of Regional Specialization vs. Spontaneous Industrial Diversity

Gershuny, J. & Fisher, K. (2014). Post-industrious society: Why work time will not disappear for our grandchildren, Center for Time Use Research, Department of Sociology, University of Oxford.

Hamel, G. (2002). Leading the Revolution: How to Thrive in Turbulent Times by Making Innovation a Way of Life, Harvard Business School Press, Boston.

Hamel, G. (2012). What matters now: How to win in a world of relentless change Ferocious Competition, and Unstoppable Innovation, John Wiley & Sons, New York.

Hannah, E.; Scott, J.; Trommer, S. (2015). Expert knowledge in Global Trade, Routledge, London.

Helfat, C. E.; Finkelstein, S.; Mitchell, W.; Peteraf, M.A.; Singh, H.; Teece, D.J. and Winter, S.G. (2007). Dynamic Capabilities: Understanding strategic change in organizations, Blackwell, Oxford.

Innerarity, D. (2012). Power and knowledge: The politics of the knowledge society, European Journal of Social Theory, 16(1), 3-16.

Jansen, J.J.P.; Van den Borch, F.A.J. & Volberda, H.W.C. (2006). Exploratory innovation, Exploitative innovation, and Performance: Effects of Organizational antecedents and environmental moderators, Management Science, 52: 1661-1674.

Jemielniak, D. (2012). The New Knowledge Workers, Edward Elgar, Cheltenham.

Johannessen, J-A.; Olsen, B. & Lumpkin, G.T. (2001). Innovation as newness: what is new, how new, and new to whom? European Journal of Innovation Management, 4,1:20-31.

Johannessen, J-A. & Olsen, B. (2010). The future of value creation and innovations: Aspects of a theory of value creation and innovation in a global knowledge economy, International Journal of Information management, Vol. 30, nr. 5: 502-511.

Johannessen, J-A. & Olsen, B. (2011). Aspect of a cybernetic theory of tacit knowledge and innovation, Kybernetes, 40, ½: 141-165.

Johannessen, J-A.; Olsen, B. & Olaisen, J. (1999). Managing and organizing innovation in the knowledge economy, European Journal of Innovation Management, 2, 3: 116-128.

Kahneman, D. (2011). *Thinking fast and slow*. New York: Allen

Lane.

Kahneman, D., & Tversky, A. (1979). An analysis of decision under risk. *Econometrica, Journal of the Econometric Society,* 47(2),263-292.

Kahneman, D., & Tversky, A. (Eds.). (2000). *Choices, values and frames.* Cambridge: Cambridge University Press.

Kahneman, D., & Tversky, A. (2008a). Prospect theory: An analysis of decision under risk, in **Kahneman, D., & Tversky, A. (Eds.) (2000b),** *Choices, values and frames* (pp. 17-43) Cambridge: Cambridge University Press..

Kanter, R. (2006). Innovation, the classic traps, Harvard Business Review, 84, 11:72-83.

Kirschbaum, R. (2005). Open innovation in practice, Research Technology Management, 48, 4:24-28.

Kirzner, I.M. (1973). Competition and entrepreneurship, The University of Chicago Press, Chicago.

Kirzner, I.M. (1979). Perception, opportunity, and profit: Studies in the theory og entrepreneurship, University of Chicago Press, Chicago.

Kirzner, I.M. (1982). The theory of entrepreneurship in economic growth; in Kent, C.A.; Sexton, D. L. and Vesper, K.H. (Ed.). Encyclopedia of Entrepreneurship, Prentice Hall, Englewood

Cliffs. N.J.

Kirzner, I.M. (1985). Discovery and the capitalist process, University of Chicago Press, Chicago.

Kirzner, I.M. (1999). Creativity and/or alertness: A reconsideration of the Schumpeterian entrepreneur, Review of Austrian Economics, 11:5-17.

Klink, R.R. & Athaide, G.A. (2006). An illustration of potential sources of concept-test error, Journal of Product Innovation Management, 23: 359-370.

Lundstrøm, A. & Stevenson, L.A. (2010). Entrepreneurship policy, theory and practice, Kluwer Academic, New York.

Maier, J. (2015). The Ambidextrous Organization: Exploring the New While Exploiting the Now, Palgrave Macmillan, New York.

Prahalad, C. K. & Krishnan, M.S. (2008). The New Age of Innovation: Driving Cocreated Value Through Global Networks, McGraw-Hill, New York.

Prahalad, C.K. & Ramaswamy, K. (2004). The future of competition, co-creating unique value with customers, Harvard Business School Press, Boston, MA.

Pyöriä, P. (2005). The Concept of Knowledge Work Revisited. Journal of Knowledge Management 9 (3): 116–127.

Ramaswamy, V. & Ozcan, K. (2014). The Co-Creation Paradigm, Stanford University Press, Stanford.

Reinhardt, W., Smith, B.; Sloep, P.Drachler, H. (2011). Knowledge Worker Roles and Actions – Results of Two Empirical Studies, Knowledge and Process Management 18 (3): 150–174.

Reinmoell, S. & Reinmoeller, P. (2015). The Ambidextrous Organization, Routledge, Oxford.

Rios, J.P. (2012). Design and Diagnoses for Sustainable Organizations, Springer, London.

Robertson, B.J. (2015). Holocracy: The Revolutionary Management System that Abolishes Hierarchy, Penguin, London.

Schumpeter, J.A. (1934). The theory of economic development, Harvard University Press, Cambridge, MA.

Shane, S. & Venkataraman,S. (2000). The promise of entrepreneurship as a field of research, Academy of Management Review, 25, 1: 217-226.

Simon, H.A. (1962). The architecture of complexity, Proceedings of the American Philosophical Society, 106: 467-482.

Simon, H.A. (1977). Models of discovery, Reidel, Boston.

Simon, H.A. (1988). Prediction and prescription in systems modelling, IASA Manuscript, Laxenburg, Austria.

Simon, H.A. (1991). Models of my life, Basic Books, New York.

Smiths, R. & Kuhlman, S. (2004). The rise of systemic instruments in innovation policy, International Journal of Foresight and Innovation Policy, 1, ½:4-32.

Stevenson, H.H. & Jarillo, J.C. (1990). A paradigm of entrepreneurship: Entrepreneurial management, Strategic Management Journal, 11:11-27.

Thomsen, E.F. (1992). Prices of knowledge: A market process perspective, Routledge, New York.

Trott, P. (2002). Innovation management and new product development, Prentice Hall, Harlow.

Urban, G.L.; Hauser, J.R.; Qualls, W.J.; Weinberg, B.D.; Bohlman, J.P. & Chicos, R.A. (1997). Information acceleration: Validation and lessons from the field, Journal of Marketing Research, 34: 47-60.

Van den Duin, P.A. ; Ortt, J.R.; Hartman, L. & Berghout, A.J. (2006). Innovation in context. In Veerburg, R.M.; Ortt, J.R. & Dicke, W.M. (Eds.) Management of technology: An introduction, Routledge, London.

Von Hippel, E. (1986). Lead users: A source of novel product concepts, Management Science, 32, 7: 791-805.

Von Hippel, E. (2005). Democratizing innovation, The Mit Press, Cambridge.

Weick, K.E. (1979). The social psychology of organizing, McGraw-Hill, New York.

White, J. & Younger, J. (2013). The Global Perspective, in Ulrich, D.; Brockbank, W.; Younger, J. & Ulrich, M. (eds.); Global HR Competencies: Mastering Competitive Value from the Outside in, McGraw Hill, New York. Pp. 27-53.

Chapter 5 New venture creation

Introduction

During the last part of the 21. century a behavioral approach in the study of entrepreneurship emerged (Collins, et.al., 2004:95-117). This was a change in the study of the entrepreneur, as it focused upon what the entrepreneur really did, instead of who he/she was (Alsos & Kolvereid, 1998). Behaviors are explicit and observable, but behind what can be demonstrated lies some knowledge processes. This knowledge processes is missed in the study of entrepreneurial behavior. We try to fill this gap in this chapter.

One may measure behavior in objective ways, but one may also loose knowledge about new venture creation when trying to measure entrepreneurial behavior. One may say that there are levels of entrepreneurial behavior, some are explicit, but others disappear when taken out and measured. Knowledge processes are some of the aspects of entrepreneurial behavior which may disappear when trying to demonstrate objectively, even if the processes behind the knowledge processes are objective, i.e. tacit knowledge processes are objective but tacit knowledge is not (Polanyi, 2009:62-92). Even if what we see is able to measure, it is not certain that we measure what we see. But, what is measured is nearly always managed. Entrepreneurial behavior is then managed and changed in relation to the so called evidence based approach, where what is measured is the objective reality. But, what if what is measured is not the objective reality, but the measured part of what we believe is reality? Then we manage entrepreneurial behavior on the basis of what we believe it to be, not what it is. Some small part of knowledge processes may be measured, but it may not be the central knowledge processes for new venture creation. Anyhow, we manage what is measured, not all of the knowledge processes used by entrepreneurs, as we try to show in this chapter.

In a knowledge approach, the entrepreneurs can learn and change as they develop their new ventures. This knowledge and learning in action is to say at least, difficult in a psychological trait approach, or even in the entrepreneurial behavior approach. Knowledge processes is not found in the entrepreneurial behavior approach during the pre-launch phase, the launch phase or the post-launch phase (Baron, 2002; Carayannis, et.al., 2015).

The entrepreneur acts on the basis of his/her basic experiences, practice and knowledge (Andersen, 2009). He/she creates something new, and sometimes destroys something old, through his/her actions (Andersen, 2011). In doing so, the entrepreneur takes a risk, which is the source of his/her profits, thereby creating uncertainty for himself/herself and others (Alsos, et.al, 2006).

In general, it is the entrepreneurial idea that drives him/her to create (Andersen, 2011). His/her ideas and knowledge often result in him/her being at odds with prevailing opinions, or the dominant logic of the market, because he/she either creates a gap in the market that changes market conditions, or he/she fills a gap in the market, exerting pressure on the competition and driving some competitors out of the market (Andersen, 2009).

The question we will examine here is: What are the knowledge conditions for new venture creation?

In attempting to answer this question, we hope to make a contribution to a policy for supporting new venture creation, in relation to both corporate entrepreneurship and independent entrepreneurship.

Figure 1 shows the elements that constitute the entrepreneurial action, as described above. Figure 1 also shows how this chapter is organized.

Figure 1 The entrepreneurial action

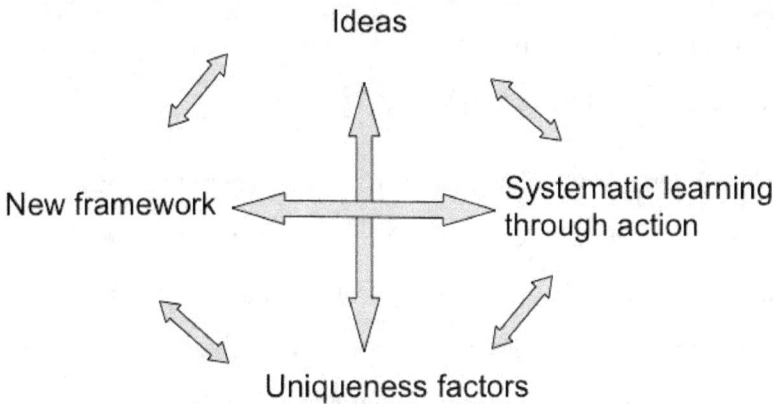

New venture creation: Setting the scene in the globalized economy

To figuratively illustrate the development of businesses during the last hundred years, we may say that there has been an evolution away from stable organizations, represented by permanently frozen pyramids, and towards fluid organizations represented by small portable tents. It is the small portable tents that may be related to the emerging Lego-structured economy – the type of economy that is evident in the global knowledge economy today (Reinhardt, et.al, 2011; Reinmoell & Reinmoeller, 2015). However, the image of small portable tents should not be misunderstood as meaning that ownership cannot be centralized; in other words, many small tents may come under the same ownership structure.

Innovation and the application of various forms of new technology make the development of agile organizations possible, illustrated metaphorically by the small portable tent that can be quickly moved around in the global knowledge economy.

This development, in which the value of basic experiences has been eroded, of necessity results to a great extent in a feeling of chaos and a loss of footing, and also possibly to a growing sense of meaninglessness (Sennett, 1998). In other words, the frozen pyramids have been melted down so that everything is now possible, but the freedom of the individual is also overwhelming, frustrating and anxiety-creating (Sennett, 2004; 2006; Baird & Henderson, 2001). The employee's feeling of solidarity with, and confidence in, organizations seems to evaporate in such a situation (Sennett, 2006:122-130; Azmat, et. al., 2012); and although the frozen pyramids characterized much of the 20th century, it now seems as if "migration is the icon of the global age, moving on rather than settling in" (Sennett, 2006: 2). In this picture new venture creation become important for job creation and economic growth (Shane & Venkataraman, 2000) and for the individuals well-being in the global knowledge economy (Azmat, et.al, 2012).

The social atomization which this development leads to, will affect all levels of society. However, there are several factors that indicate that this will lead to greater economic growth (Sennett, 2006) but at a high price, namely "greater economic inequality as well as social instability" (Sennett, 2006:3). Both social inequality and social instability may lead to migration (Sennett, 2006). At the level of the individual, Sennett (2006:4) says there are three challenges that will be important to deal with:

1. How are we to deal with temporary employment relations?
2. How do we develop new skills when we do not know what will be in demand tomorrow?
3. How do we cope with the future given the collapse of the relevance of our basic experiences?

If we fail to respond satisfactorily to these questions, then resignation, passivity, uncertainty and the fear of being made redundant by the ongoing radical changes could easily be the result (Sennett, 2006). One way out of these dilemmas, we think, is an energized focus on new venture creation.

One of the consequences which Sennett points out, as we see it, is that individuals must take greater responsibility for their own careers and futures, i.e. new venture creation. Another consequence of this development may be that the authority and status of the leader of the hierarchical organization will crumble, amongst other things, because the people they lead will search for other career paths, for example in entrepreneurial activities. Authority, status and titles are likely to come to mean less as mobility increases, as more and more people will see the scope of opportunity that opens up in the global knowledge economy, enabling them to create something for themselves through new venture creation.

Knowledge processes at the organizational level

An essential aspect of innovation and entrepreneurship is the individual's ability to use more knowledge than he/she possesses to promote his/her projects (Hayek, 1978: 22). Knowledge is generally divided into two main categories: explicit, which can be codified, and tacit knowledge, which can not be codified. Explicit knowledge can be relatively easily formulated using words, figures and symbols, and it can be digitized. This knowledge can then relatively easily be transmitted to others, for example, by the use of ICT. Tacit knowledge is rooted in action (practice) and is connected to specific contexts (Polanyi, 2009; Welsh & Lyons, 2001). This knowledge is difficult to communicate to others as information, and cannot be digitized. Tacit knowledge is often the most important strategic resource for many companies, since it is difficult for others to imitate, and rooted in the specific problems a company is set to solve (Hannah, et.al., 2015). Tacit knowledge can thus be described as an important strategic capability for companies (Helfat, et.al., 2007).

In addition to these two types of knowledge, there are two other kinds of knowledge that have become increasingly important: hidden knowledge (see Kirzner, 1973; 1979;1982; Grant, 2003;

2012) and implicit knowledge (Shanks, 1997:197-215; Hayek, 1978).

Hidden knowledge may be termed what we do not know that we do not know; and as several claim, it is the basis for creativity and innovation (Kirzner, 1982: 273), or "the management of ignorance" which is "the key issue for companies as it is for society" (Grant, 2003: 222). Kirzner (1982: 273) states explicitly with regard to this type of knowledge that it is where the opportunity for what is creative and new can be found, saying, "people do not know what it is that they do not know".

Implicit knowledge is the knowledge possessed by organizations, but which is not utilised and put into productive practice because of knowledge boundaries. Therefore, organizations are "dumber than they need to be", in that they do not exploit this potential (Pfeffer, 2007). Explicit, tacit, hidden and implicit types of knowledge may be developed through collective learning processes within the company.

From a knowledge perspective, entrepreneurship conditions consist of the following knowledge processes:

1. Explicit knowledge, i.e. what we know and can be digitized.
2. Tacit knowledge, i.e. the knowledge you have difficulty in transferring to others as information (Polanyi,1958; 2009).

3. Hidden knowledge, i.e. what people do not know that they do not know (see Kirzner, 1982:272).
4. Implicit knowledge, i.e. what people know that they do not know, and therefore need assistance in addressing (see Hayek, 1978:22).

One of the unintended consequences of rational planning is the limiting of the area of knowledge, because it is based, almost per definition, on explicit knowledge. Consequently, implicit knowledge, to a large extent tacit knowledge, and certainly hidden knowledge are at best de-emphasized, and at worst absent from the entrepreneurial policy formulations. The effect of placing more emphasis on explicit knowledge in the entrepreneurship process results in a narrowing of the inspiration for entrepreneurial action, because the scope of opportunity is limited and a smaller part of the knowledge we actually possess is used.

If developers of entrepreneurship policy at various levels only choose to base their policy on some of the types of knowledge available, for instance, on explicit and tacit knowledge, this may inhibit entrepreneurial actions. In the context of policy, it is therefore not a question of what knowledge the entrepreneur possesses, but rather a question of which view of knowledge policy developers have.

The idea we have tried to convey here is that explicit knowledge constitutes only a small part of the area of knowledge that results in new venture creation. Explicit knowledge is largely linked to the formal education system, planning, business plans, control functions to ensure the business plan is implemented, etc.

Implicit knowledge requires participation in, and understanding of, how networks function. Tacit knowledge requires learning through a master-apprentice system, where practice is given priority over theory. Hidden knowledge presupposes an open and questioning mind and a creative imagination, that is, insight into creative processes.

Every organization relies to varying degrees on explicit, implicit, hidden and tacit knowledge. Implicit knowledge is expressed in the statement that organizations know more knowledge than they use, and are therefore more ignorant than they need to be (see Pfeffer, 2007). The basis of implicit knowledge can be found in the following expression in Hayek (1980: 14): "… the fact that he cannot know more than a tiny part of the whole of society and that therefore all that can enter into his motives are the immediate effects which his actions will have in the sphere he knows".

The individual entrepreneur's knowledge is limited, and, consequently, the connections made between the knowledge that different people possess may lead to a greater scope of opportunities, both for the entrepreneur and the social system the entrepreneur is a part of. This is what the function of implicit knowledge is – sharing in order to receive more than one gives. Implicit knowledge may be said to be contextual knowledge at the collective level, or "connected action cooperation" (von Mises, 1996:143).

That which cannot be foreseen or predicted will, Hayek argues (1978: 29), be best managed by allowing the individual maximum freedom of action. However, the individual entrepreneur prepares himself/herself constantly for that which he/she knows nothing about, that which emerges within the scope of opportunities.

It is probably not the case that chance and luck are as random as we tend to believe; it is probably more the case, as Louis Pasteur expressed it, that chance and luck are attracted by the person who is well prepared (see Taton, 1957: 91).

Preparation consists of the individual entrepreneur being able to freely seek knowledge through open networks, thereby reducing the ignorance that arises when one limits the room for action of the individual (see Hayek, 1978: 29). Ignorance seems also to be institutionalized when knowledge processes are organized through a hierarchical command and control system, using mostly explicit knowledge. This insight was formulated by Kline & Martin (1958: 70) fifty years ago in the following way: "the chief characteristic[…] of the command hierarchy … is not knowledge but ignorance."

One of the implications is that the more restrictions you place on the entrepreneurial action, the less grasp the entrepreneur will have of what is going on in the other knowledge domains. The entrepreneur will thus become disconnected from areas of knowledge when creating something new. In this way, ignorance becomes institutionalized, instead of increasing the area of knowledge. Depending on how the social system is organized, the area of knowledge available for entrepreneurial action is either increased or decreased.

We cannot expect to achieve any form of certainty through entrepreneurial actions, but we can ensure that the room of action is extended as far as possible, by limiting institutionalized ignorance, so that the entrepreneurial action has the greatest probability of success.

As a general rule, most people act on the basis of the knowledge they possess; anything else would be perceived as "contrary to intelligent action" (Hayek, 1978: 34). However, the entrepreneur acts, to a great extent, not on the basis of his/her explicit knowledge, but rather by using implicit knowledge, which by definition is created outside the individual's area of expertise, or by reaching towards hidden knowledge, the areas where you do not even know what you do not know (Kirzner, 1982:272). By performing these acts based on areas of implicit and hidden knowledge, the entrepreneur opens up opportunities no one else has access to.

Against this background, the entrepreneurial action is often considered irrational as far as explicit knowledge is concerned, because explicit knowledge uses clear rules, procedures, data, facts and probable assertions. Consequently, the results of the entrepreneurial action are in many cases regarded as chance and luck, while in reality they are the result of the entrepreneur being able to reach out to domains of knowledge beyond explicit knowledge.

We have shown the area of knowledge for new venture creation in Figure 2

Figure 2 The area of entrepreneurial knowledge

Knowledge types \ Knowledging	Development of knowledge	Mobilization of knowledge	Integration of knowledge	Coordination of knowledge
Tacit knowledge	Practical contexts	Mentoring	Master-apprentice relationships	Organization
Explicit knowledge	Systematic cognitive processes	Clear intentions	Experience transference	Results focus
Implicit knowledge	Structural relations	Networks	Multi-disciplinary teams	Clear aims
Hidden knowledge	Columbus strategies	Innovation processes	Entrepreneurship	Incentives

Proposition 1: At the policy level all four types of knowledge and their conditions should be taken into account in order to promote new venture creation.

Organizational implications: Once the scope of opportunity is maximized, and we allow elements of knowledge that did not previously interact with each other to come into contact, then spontaneous ideas may emerge, which have in them the ability to enable the creation of something new.

The entrepreneurial action is always performed by one or more people, acting alone or in interaction with others. The result of the entrepreneurial action is often greater uncertainty for some. The entrepreneur takes the risk, we say, and acts in an environment characterized by uncertainty.

The next section will discuss new venture creation in the context of risk and uncertainty.

Policy level: Risk and uncertainty

New venture creation is always directed towards the future. The action aims to change future conditions and requirements, and in this way the entrepreneurial action creates uncertainty.

Not only does the entrepreneurial action create uncertainty, it also operates in an unknown future. Von Mises (1996:106) says on this point: "It is in this sense always a risky speculation."

Risk is linked to uncertainty and ambiguity. The uncertainty is moderated by information, but can never be removed, primarily because it is impossible to obtain information about the domain of tacit and hidden knowledge. Ambiguity may be reduced by communication; however, communication creates new ambiguity, because different people will interpret emerging events and actions in different ways.

In this context, risk is viewed as an abstraction, while uncertainty relates to what is concrete. Von Mises expresses the following (1996: 809): "A popular fallacy considers entrepreneurial profit a reward for risk-taking." The entrepreneur takes no more risks than the individual capitalist. In other words, the distinction between risk and uncertainty is that risk is at the level of abstraction. Risk relates to the class of entrepreneurial actions, whereas uncertainty relates to the individual entrepreneurial action. Risk may be calculated statistically; however, statistical calculation cannot be applied to an individual entrepreneurial action. The confusion between risk and uncertainty can easily occur because the two words are almost synonymous in everyday language. However, to reiterate: when we talk about entrepreneurial risk, we are referring to risk associated with **the class of** entrepreneurial actions.

Von Mises (1996: 106-116), referring to Knight (1921), who was the first economist to make an analytical distinction between risk and uncertainty, considers risk to be a concept linked to the probability of a whole class of events, such as an entrepreneurial action. Uncertainty, however, is linked to specific cases, such as individual entrepreneurial actions. Uncertainty cannot be assessed from any probability calculation. This is where explicit knowledge, tacit knowledge, implicit knowledge and hidden knowledge are applicable. Uncertainty cannot be calculated, whereas risk can for any class of events.

Proposition 2: Risk can be calculated from the degree of knowledge about the class of an event.

Policy implications: Risk may be expressed with regard to the probability for an entire class of events, such as a class of entrepreneurial actions.

Proposition 3: Uncertainty relates to information and knowledge concerning an individual entrepreneurial action.

Policy implications: Uncertainty is reduced by information.

Reflection upon risk and uncertainty in relation to new venture creation

The following section discusses Schumpeter's view of risk and uncertainty in relation to entrepreneurship. For Schumpeter, entrepreneurship and innovation are two sides of same coin – both help to explain, and are necessary, for economic growth. The independent entrepreneur was for the early Schumpeter (1934) the fundamental driving force in economic development. Without the entrepreneur, the economic system could be regarded more as a circular process, says Schumpeter (1934:61): "running in channels essentially the same year after year – similar to the circulation of the blood in an animal organism". The entrepreneur initiates processes, says Schumpeter, which then result in creative destruction at different levels in the economic system. *This*, says

Schumpeter, makes the comparison with the blood circulation in animal organisms useless as a metaphor for an economic system.

The innovative entrepreneur creates something new that has never been seen before in the world. He/she does this, for instance, by trying out new combinations, which takes him/her into the unknown where uncertainty reigns. In this way, the economic system is driven forward not as a struggle between capital and labour as Karl Marx believed, but as a continuous tension between new ideas and *contrapreneurs*. The contrapreneurs are those who are satisfied with the status quo; consequently, contrapreneurs may belong to both labor and capital in the Marxian sense. This suggests that the struggle between capital and labor does not necessarily bring the system forward, but may equally be used to maintain the status quo.

Creative destruction, the destruction of the old and the emergence of the new after small or large "forest fires", leads to established experiences – i.e. the data you have used, the rules and procedures you have applied – no longer being applicable. The reliance on basic experiences collapses during the process of creative destruction. The degree of creative destruction and the consequences of the destruction vary with the degree of the innovations introduced into the market. In such situations uncertainty is the only certain element.

The entrepreneurial action can cause losses, or result in an extraordinary profit. If there were no innovative entrepreneurial actions, then as mentioned above, the economy could be compared to the circulation of blood in biological organisms, "essentially the same year after year" (Schumpeter, 1934: 61).

When Schumpeter (1934:137) states that: "the entrepreneur is never the risk bearer", the meaning of the word "risk" may be interpreted on an abstract level. Knight (1921), says that risk is linked to a class of actions, not to the individual actions.

Of course, in everyday language the meaning of the word "risk" would render Schumpeter's statement meaningless. In addition, it is not particularly useful to distinguish between the entrepreneur and the capitalist, as Schumpeter (1954: 556) does, if this is a reference to independent entrepreneurs. However, in the context of 1954, Schumpeter's statement most probably refers to corporate entrepreneurship. In his later work Schumpeter was mainly concerned with this type of entrepreneurship, i.e. the intrapreneurs in large enterprises. In such a context, it makes sense to say the capitalist takes the risk, not the entrepreneur.

If we had complete information and perfect knowledge, there would still be considerable uncertainty associated with new venture creation, due to the presence of hidden knowledge (Kizner, 1982:272), which could turn up like a creative Jack-in-the-box, bringing new uncertainty. In other words, the nature of knowledge is such that new knowledge is continuously created from, amongst other things, hidden knowledge (Kirzner, 1973; 1979; 1985; 1999).

In this context, uncertainty may be defined as a situation in which there is a large possibility of losing something that means something to yourself or others. These potential losses may relate to income, investment, reputation, trust, etc.

In everyday language we say that those who start up a business take risks, because the probability of success is relatively small. When we know from research that the likelihood of success is small, why does an entrepreneur try to start a business? One explanation could be that they have higher expectations of success than is shown by the statistics (Cooper et al. 1988). Cooper et.al. found in their survey carried out in the US that 95% of the entrepreneurs thought they would succeed, while in fact only 50% actually succeeded. They used data from 2994 independent entrepreneurs. A second explanation may be that the entrepreneur is a role model in today's society, and entrepreneurial action is often executed by those people wishing to emulate a role model. A third and simple explanation may be that this is one of the few opportunities an individual has to achieve large gains, which he/she would not otherwise be able to achieve, for instance as an employee. A fourth explanation may be related to the prospect theory (Kahneman, 2011; Kahneman & Tversky, 1979; 2000). In this theory, the entrepreneur is driven by a burning desire to move from a position below the average income to a position far above the average. A fifth explanation may be that entrepreneurs are more willing to take risks than those who do not start new businesses (McGrath, et al., 1992). What we do know, however, with relatively great certainty, is that it is unlikely that this is correct, at least when comparing entrepreneurs with leaders of large enterprises. There are no statistical differences in risk-taking found between the two groups (Low & MacMillan, 1988). A sixth explanation is that the entrepreneur has a limited knowledge of the risk, or does not see the risk involved in the entrepreneurial action. This explanation implies that the entrepreneur is not necessarily intending to take more risk than others, but rather does not know enough about the risks (Busenitz & Barney, 1997; Simon et al., 1999).

Proposition 4: The innovative entrepreneur brings the economic system forward, because he creates creative destructions at many levels where the productivity is low.

Policy implications: Innovations promote small and big economic crises, because the old is destructed and it takes time before the new is in production.

Methodological implications

Creative chaos has as its main purpose the development of hidden knowledge in organizations (Kirzner, 1973;1979;1982;1985;1999). In this process, various creative strategies, methods and techniques are used, among other things ambidextrous organizing and system four developed in Beers viable system model (Beer, 1995), named here as "an eye towards the future".

Tacit knowledge is developed and transmitted through various master-apprentice schemes and structured mentoring. Skills are often linked to tacit knowledge, the kind of knowledge that is difficult to convey to others as "information" (Polanyi, 1958; 2009).

Explicit knowledge is developed through research, training, education and the development and design of early warning systems, trends and lifestyle analyses (Mayer, 2015). In bringing out implicit knowledge, the knowledge that exists within the organization, the knowledge you have not been introduced to– to put it figuratively – there are in principle two ways of engaging with this knowledge. First, continual change processes are needed, so that expertise always challenges new boundaries (Ramaswamy & Ozcan, 2014). In practice this means that regular reorganization is important, because new areas of expertise will be forced to connect with each other. In this way, more new areas of expertise will become steadily integrated, and the organization will exploit an increasingly larger part of its potential. Second, the integration of knowledge in the global knowledge economy requires decentralization and an extreme front-line focus. A front-line focus has two purposes. At a time of major changes, businesses need to make decisions quickly. Drucker (1994: 80), amongst others, says such decisions: "must be based on closeness to performance, to the market, to technology, and to the many changes in society, the environment, demographics..." In this context, the front-line focus is connected to the closeness between a business and its customers, users and other critical stakeholders. Those on the front line should have access to information, have the necessary decision-making authority, and always be at the forefront of their field of expertise.

Methodology proposition 1: To bring forward implicit knowledge set in motion continual change processes, and create a front line focus.

Methodology proposition 2: To bring forward explicit knowledge, create and set in motion trend analysis, early warning systems, internal education of employees, and R&D systems.

Methodology proposition 3: To bring forward tacit knowledge create and set in motion structured mentor arrangements, and organize along the lines of master/apprentice programs.

Methodology proposition 4: To bring forward hidden knowledge organize creative chaos with focus on the organizing principle that lies behind "an eye towards the future".

Conclusion

The research question in this chapter was: What are the knowledge conditions for new venture creation? The short answer is that the foundation for entrepreneurial action lies upon four types of knowledge: explicit knowledge, tacit knowledge, implicit knowledge and hidden knowledge.

The deeper answer to the research question is stated in the mini-theory developed through this chapter represented in five propositions with implications and four methodological propositions.

The practical answer to the research question is linked to the four methodologies developed in order to bring forward the four types of knowledge types discussed in this chapter.

There ought to be empirical research linking entrepreneurial action to the four types of knowledge discussed in this chapter. First a case study should be done. Then a longitudinal case study would strengthen the insights between the four knowledge types and entrepreneurship. The underlying proposition in this chapter, which should be investigated, is that if we know more about the connection between entrepreneurship and the four knowledge types, then it would be easier to lay the foundation for entrepreneurial success.

Bibliography

Alsos, G.A. & Kolvereid, L. (1998). The Business Gestation Process of Novice, Serial, and Parallel Business Founders, Entrepreneurship, Theory and Practice, 22, 4: 101-114.

Alsos, G.; Isaksen, E.J. & Ljungren, E. (2006). New Venture Business Growth in Men-Women-Led Businesses, Entrepreneurship Theory and Practice, 30, 5:667-686.

Andersen, E. (2009). Schumpeter's Evolutionary Economics: A Theoretical, Historical and Statistical Analysis of the Engine of Capitalism, Anthem Press, London.

Andersen, E.S (2011). Joseph A. Schumpeter: A Theory of Social and Economic Evolution (Great Thinkers in Economics), Palgrave, London.

Azmat, G.; Manning, A. & Van Reenen, J. (2012). Privatization and the Decline of the Labour's Share: International Evidence from Network Industries, Economica, 79:470-492.

Baird,L. & Henderson, J.C. (2001). The Knowledge Engine, Berrett-Koehler, San Francisco.

Baron, R.A. (2002). OB and entrepreneurship: The reciprocal benefits of closer conceptual links, Research in Organizational Behavior, 24:225-269.

Beer, S. (1995). Diagnosing the system for organizing, John Wiley & Sons, New York.

Bennis, W. & Slatter, W. (1968). The Temporary Society, Jossey-Bass, San Francisco.

Bunge, M. (1998). Philosophy of science: From problem to theory, Volume one, Transaction Publishers, New Jersey.

Busenitz, L.W. & Barney, J.B. (1997). Differences between entrepreneurs and managers in large organizations: Biases and heuristics in strategic decision-making, Journal of Business Venturing, 12: 9-30.

Carayannis, E.G.; Samara, E.T. & Bokouros, Y.L. (2015). Innovation and entrepreneurship: Theory, policy and practice, Springer, Berlin.

Collins, C.J.; Hanges, P.J. & Locke, E.A. (2004). The relationship of achievement motivation to entrepreneurial behavior: A Meta-analysis, Human Performance, 17, 1:95-117.

Cooper, A.C.; Woo, C.Y. & Dunkelberg, W.C. (1988). "Entrepreneurs perceived chances of success", Journal of Business Venturing, 3: 97-108.

Drucker, P.F. (1994). Managing in turbulent times, Routledge,

London.

Grant, R.M. (2003). The Knowledge-Based View of the Firm, i Faulkner, D. & Campell, A. (red.). The Oxford Handbook of Strategy, Oxford University Press, Oxford. S. 203-231.

Grant, R.M. (2012). Contemporary Strategy Analysis, John Wiley & Sons, New York.

Hannah, E.; Scott, J.; Trommer, S. (2015). Expert knowledge in Global Trade, Routledge, London.

Helfat, C. E.; Finkelstein, S.; Mitchell, W.; Peteraf, M.A.; Singh, H.; Teece, D.J. and Winter, S.G. (2007). Dynamic Capabilities: Understanding strategic change in organizations, Blackwell, Oxford.

Hayek, F.A. (1978). The Constitution of Liberty, The University of Chicago Press, Chicago.

Hayek, F.A. (1980). Individualism and Economic Order, The University of Chicago Press, Chicago.

Kahneman, D. (2011). *Thinking fast and slow*. New York: Allen Lane.

Kahneman, D., & Tversky, A. (1979). An analysis of decision under risk. *Econometrica,*

Journal of the Econometric Society, 47(2), 263-292.

Kahneman, D., & Tversky, A. (2000). Prospect theory: An analysis of decision under risk.

In D. Kahneman, & A. Tversky (Eds.), *Choices, values and frames* (pp. 17-43)Cambridge:

Cambridge University Press.

Kirzner, I.M. (1973). Competition and entrepreneurship, The University of Chicago Press, Chicago.

Kirzner, I.M. (1979). Perception, opportunity, and profit: Studies in the theory og entrepreneurship, University of Chicago Press, Chicago.

Kirzner, I.M. (1982). The theory of entrepreneurship in economic growth; in Kent, C.A.; Sexton, D. L. and Vesper, K.H. (Ed.). Encyclopedia of Entrepreneurship, Prentice Hall, Englewood Cliffs. N.J.

Kirzner, I.M. (1985). Discovery and the capitalist process, University of Chicago Press, Chicago.

Kirzner, I.M. (1999). Creativity and/or alertness: A reconsideration of the Schumpeterian entrepreneur, Review of Austrian Economics, 11:5-17.

Kline, B.E. & Martin, N.H. (1958). Freedom, Authority and Decentralization, Harvard Business Review.

Knight, F.H. (1921). Risk, Uncertainty and Profit, Harper, New

York.

Low, M.B. & MacMillan, I.C. (1988). Entrepreneurship: Past research and future challenges, Journal of Management, 14, 2: 139-161.

Maier, J. (2015). The Ambidextrous Organization: Exploring the New While Exploiting the Now, Palgrave Macmillan, New York.

McGrath, R.G.; MacMillan, I.C. & Scheinberg, S. (1992). "Elitists, risk-taking, and rugged individualists? An exploratory analysis of cultural differences between entrepreneurs and non-entrepreneurs", Journal of Business Venturing, 7: 115-135.

Polanyi, M. (1958). Personal knowledge, Routledge & Kegan Paul, London.

Polanyi, M. (2009). The tacit dimention, The University of Chicago Press, Chicago.

Pfeffer, J. (2007). What were They Thinking, Harvard Business School Press, Boston.

Ramaswamy, V. & Ozcan, K. (2014). The Co-Creation Paradigm, Stanford University Press, Stanford.

Reinhardt, W., Smith, B.; Sloep, P.Drachler, H. (2011). Knowledge Worker Roles and Actions – Results of Two Empirical Studies, Knowledge and Process Management 18 (3): 150–174.

Reinmoell, S. & Reinmoeller, P. (2015). The Ambidextrous Organization, Routledge, Oxford.

Schumpeter, J.A. (1934). The Theory of Economic Development, Cambridge, Mass.

Schumpeter, J.A. (1954). History of Economic Analysis, London.

Sennett, R. (1998). The Corrosion of Character, Norton, New York.

Sennett, R. (2004). Respect, Norton, New York.

Sennett, R. (2006). The Culture of the New Capitalism, Yale University Press, London.

Shane, S. & Venkataraman,S. (2000). The promise of entrepreneurship as a field of research, Academy of Management Review, 25, 1: 217-226.

Shanks, D.R. (1997). Distributed representations and implicit knowledge, I Lamberts, K. & Shanks, D. (1997). Knowledge, concepts and categories, Psycology Press, London. S. 197-215.

Simon, M.; Houghton, S.M. & Savelli, S. (2003). "Out of the frying pan? Why small business managers introduce high-risk products", Journal of Business Venturing, 18: 419-440.

Taton, R. (1957). Reason and Chance in Scientific Discovery, London.

von Mises, L. (1996). Human Action, Bettina Bien Greaves, San Francisco (First edition 1949).

Welsh, I. & Lyons, M. (2001). Evidence-based care and the case for intuition and tacit knowledge in clinical assessment and decision making in mental health nursing practice: an empirical contribution to the debate, Journal of Psychiatric andMental Health Nursing, 8, 4:299-305

Introduction to innovation Vol. 2

Index

"

"Corporate" entrepreneurship, 11

A

Assumptions, 51

B

Bunge, 38, 121, 151, 186
bureaucratic, 7, 36, 61, 146
business models, 40, 57

C

context, 8, 9, 17, 55, 59, 68, 73, 77, 94, 95, 96, 97, 99, 102, 103, 106, 108, 112, 114, 118, 120, 129, 142, 158, 169, 174, 176, 179, 180, 183
creative, 8, 9, 13, 14, 23, 24, 27, 33, 34, 35, 50, 53, 55, 59, 69, 79, 94, 130, 142, 149, 168, 170, 177, 178, 179, 181, 183
creative destruction, 9, 13, 23, 27, 69, 130, 177, 178
creativity, 14, 24, 31, 50, 52, 115, 118, 141, 168

D

Deutero-learning, 108, 109
double loop learning, 98, 115, 118

E

entrepreneur, 7, 8, 11, 12, 17, 18, 19, 20, 21, 22, 23, 26, 128, 130, 131, 132, 152, 156, 161, 162, 169, 170, 171, 172, 173, 174, 176, 177, 179, 180, 188
entrepreneurs, 7, 8, 11, 17, 23, 26, 48, 128, 130, 162, 179, 180, 186, 189
entrepreneurship, v, 6, 7, 8, 9, 10, 11, 12, 13, 14, 15, 16, 17, 18, 19, 21, 22, 23, 24, 25, 26, 27, 31, 33, 34, 35, 38, 39, 40, 41, 42, 43, 44, 46, 47, 48, 49, 85, 127, 128, 129, 130, 131, 132, 133, 135, 137, 140, 141, 142, 143, 144, 145, 146, 147, 148, 149, 151, 155, 157, 158, 161, 163, 167, 168, 169, 177, 179, 184, 185, 186, 188, 190
equilibrium, 8, 27, 130, 131
explicit, 25, 49, 55, 56, 58, 79, 80, 92, 94, 95, 98, 112, 118, 121, 125, 131, 137, 161, 167, 169, 170, 171, 172, 176, 183, 184

F

feedback, 59, 61, 64, 65, 116, 135, 148
feedforward, 148
flexibility, 19, 29, 90

G

global, 28, 29, 32, 57, 58, 60, 102, 137, 149, 154, 164, 165, 166, 182

H

Hidden knowledge, 24, 50, 52, 55, 56, 58, 66, 71, 75, 79, 143, 168, 170
hierarchical, 36, 145, 146, 166, 171
Holistic, 107, 108, 115
hot spot, 12, 13

I

ideas, 13, 14, 19, 22, 31, 56, 57, 58, 59, 60, 61, 62, 63, 64, 65, 71, 78, 112, 128, 131, 135, 136, 137, 142, 163, 174, 178
Implicit knowledge, 50, 168, 169, 170

innovation, i, v, 8, 9, 15, 23, 24, 26, 27, 29, 31, 35, 36, 42, 49, 50, 51, 52, 53, 57, 58, 60, 64, 84, 91, 92, 93, 99, 102, 109, 114, 115, 116, 117, 118, 121, 122, 123, 127, 128, 129, 130, 131, 132, 133, 134, 135, 136, 137, 140, 141, 142, 143, 144, 145, 146, 147, 148, 149, 151, 152, 154, 155, 158, 159, 167, 168, 177

innovative entrepreneur, 7, 178, 181

innovative entrepreneurship, 11, 145

interaction, 55, 96, 102, 129, 132, 135, 137, 143, 144, 146, 148, 149, 174

intrapreneur, 12, 18, 19, 21, 22

intrapreneurial, 6, 9, 10, 11, 13, 14, 16, 22, 23, 26, 33, 34, 35, 36, 37, 128

intrapreneurial intensity, 7, 13, 34, 36, 37

intrapreneurs, 11, 12, 17, 179

intrapreneurship, 8, 12, 34, 128

intuition, 101, 102, 111, 113, 118, 121, 123, 125, 126, 131, 140, 142, 191

K

Knowledge, v, 7, 38, 40, 47, 49, 82, 85, 86, 88, 91, 120, 122, 124, 125, 150, 154, 156, 157, 161, 162, 167, 185, 187, 189, 190

knowledge economy, 28, 29, 32, 33, 42, 58, 60, 137, 149, 154, 164, 165, 166, 182

knowledge-logic, 30

L

learning by doing, 98, 111, 116, 117, 119, 120, 125

linear model, 134, 147

M

management, v, 6, 11, 13, 14, 15, 16, 28, 30, 31, 39, 40, 42, 44, 50, 56, 58, 59, 60, 61, 62, 63, 64, 65, 84, 90, 91, 99, 101, 112, 118, 120, 121, 122, 125, 141, 145, 154, 158, 168

models, 13, 20, 40, 57, 60, 63, 64, 65, 127, 128, 129, 131, 133, 135, 140, 141, 143, 147, 149

modular logic, 29

O

organization, 7, 9, 13, 14, 16, 22, 30, 31, 32, 33, 35, 36, 43, 50, 52, 53, 55, 56, 58, 59, 60, 61, 62, 63, 64, 65, 71, 72, 73, 75, 77, 78, 79, 80, 84, 119, 124, 136, 140, 142, 143, 146, 147, 166, 170, 182

organizational, 7, 13, 14, 36, 49, 51, 53, 80, 85, 86, 92, 93, 99, 103, 104, 105, 114, 117, 118, 121, 122, 123, 124, 125, 127, 128, 133, 144, 145, 147, 149, 167

P

paradox, 24

perception, 100, 111, 138

phenomenon, 95, 96, 97, 109, 116

practical knowledge, 99, 102, 107

punctuated, 108

R

reflection, 52, 53, 54, 55, 95, 96, 97, 136, 143

reputation, 31, 180

S

single loop learning, 98

social system, 51, 52, 96, 170, 172

strategic, 6, 8, 9, 10, 11, 13, 14, 15, 16, 18, 19, 21, 22, 25, 26, 28, 30, 31, 33, 34, 35, 39, 40, 42, 43, 50, 90,

102, 103, 113, 118, 128, 137, 153, 167, 186, 187
strategic entrepreneurship, 6, 8, 10, 13, 14, 15, 25, 128
Strategic management, 14
Strategy, 39, 40, 46, 48, 52, 53, 56, 57, 68, 70, 84, 89, 187
system, 6, 9, 11, 13, 22, 27, 28, 34, 51, 52, 53, 55, 56, 65, 69, 97, 100, 107, 108, 110, 113, 114, 116, 129, 144, 146, 170, 171, 177, 178, 181, 182, 186

T

tacit, 25, 49, 55, 58, 59, 79, 80, 92, 93, 95, 96, 97, 98, 99, 100, 101, 102, 104, 105, 106, 107, 108, 111, 112, 114, 115, 116, 117, 118, 119, 120, 121, 122, 123, 124, 126, 131, 132, 142, 154, 161, 167, 168, 169, 170, 175, 176, 182, 183, 184, 189, 191
tacit knowledge, 59, 79, 92, 94, 95, 96, 97, 98, 99, 100, 101, 102, 103, 104, 108, 111, 114, 115, 116, 117, 118, 125, 131, 132, 161
theory, 6, 22, 34, 37, 38, 43, 51, 52, 53, 81, 83, 85, 119, 121, 122, 124, 127, 140, 144, 151, 152, 154, 155, 156, 157, 170, 180, 184, 186, 188

V

value chain, 27, 28, 29, 30, 31
value dialogue, 27, 31, 33, 35
value network, 27, 29, 31
value shop, 27, 30
value-creation, 6

ABOUT THE AUTHORS

Adriaenssen, D. is cand. Psychol., Århus University, Denmark.

Johannessen is professor (full) at Kristiania University College, and Nord University, Norway.

Skålsvik, H., is associate professor, The Artic University, Norway.

Stokvik, H., is assistant professor, Nord University, Norway

Sætesdahl,H., is associate professor, and Dean, at Kristiania University College, Norway.

www.ingramcontent.com/pod-product-compliance
Lightning Source LLC
Chambersburg PA
CBHW071812200526
45169CB00017B/189